William Albert Andrews

A Daring Voyage Across the Atlantic Ocean

By two Americans, the brothers Andrews: the log of the voyage

William Albert Andrews

A Daring Voyage Across the Atlantic Ocean
By two Americans, the brothers Andrews: the log of the voyage

ISBN/EAN: 9783337037925

Printed in Europe, USA, Canada, Australia, Japan

Cover: Foto ©Andreas Hilbeck / pixelio.de

More available books at **www.hansebooks.com**

BY
TWO AMERICANS, THE BROTHERS ANDREWS.

THE "NAUTILUS."
19 *feet long*, 6 *feet* 7 *inches wide*, 2 *feet* 3 *inches deep*.

THE LOG OF THE VOYAGE BY CAPTAIN WILLIAM A. ANDREWS.

WITH INTRODUCTION AND NOTES BY DR. MACAULAY,
EDITOR OF "THE BOY'S OWN PAPER."

NEW YORK:
E. P. DUTTON AND CO.
GRIFFITH AND FARRAN, ST. PAUL'S CHURCHYARD, LONDON.
MDCCCLXXX.

CONTENTS.

CHAPTER I.
THE FIRST IDEA OF THE VOYAGE 1

CHAPTER II.
CROSSING THE ATLANTIC 5

CHAPTER III.
PERILS OF THE ATLANTIC 17

CHAPTER IV.
PERILS OF THE "NAUTILUS" AND CREW . . . 39

CHAPTER V.
THE LOG OF THE "NAUTILUS" 47

CHAPTER VI.
REMARKS ON THE LOG 131

A DARING VOYAGE
ACROSS THE ATLANTIC.

CHAPTER I.

The First Idea of the Voyage.

It was a splendid afternoon in the month of September, 1877. Two brothers, William A. Andrews and Asa Walter Andrews, were seated on the cliffs above the entrance of Beverly Harbour, in New England. A refreshing breeze was blowing from the south, and wafting numerous small boats on the waters before them in every direction. It was a delightful locality, on the brow of a bluff, and the scene unexcelled by any on the eastern coast of America. On the left was the pleasant rural residence of the Burgess family, while on the right, across the entrance to the harbour, was the well-known Juniper Point, with Lowell Camp, a favourite holiday resort. Here Boston men, and many others, are wont to repair for rest and change from the toils and troubles of business life—boating, bathing, fishing, cooking their own meals, and otherwise enjoying a time of recreation.

Gazing from the height out on to the broad Atlantic, beyond the numerous islands on the coast, one of the brothers broke a long silence by saying to the other, " Let us cross the old ocean in one of these Dories,"—pointing down to a number of boats that lay moored almost under where they were sitting.

" Give me your hand," said the other, " I'll go with you;" and they shook hands, agreeing to make the voyage.

It was a sudden impulse, but the purpose was formed, and they kept to it. They resolved to wait till the following year, and to start in June, which was thought the best time for so great a voyage. The winter would afford leisure for preparation, and especially for perfecting such knowledge of navigation as would suffice for the undertaking.

In May of the next year, 1878, a boat was ordered, and built by Higgins and Gifford, famous builders at Gloucester, Massachusetts. The name "Nautilus" was chosen by the elder brother, who said in a letter to the editor of *The Boy's Own Paper*, "I understand it is a Greek word signifying a miniature ship. It is from their resemblance to miniature ships that the nautilus of naturalists has its name. They have but one sail, and what might be construed to represent oars (their appendages); so it was suggestive to me to name my boat after them. There was a boat in Boston at the time of the same name, which had met with various accidents, and was always in trouble of some kind. The thought often crossed my mind that it was therefore an unlucky name. But my general disbelief in such superstitious ideas soon overcame that prejudice, and we resolved that, come what would, this should be its appellation. Jules Verne, in his 'Twenty Thousand Leagues under the Sea,' also named the nondescript vessel of his fertile imagination although of no resemblance in the least), the Nautilus." So the name was fixed, and the boat was at Boston ready for the voyage.

CHAPTER II.

Crossing the Atlantic.

Merchant ships and mail steamers are crossing the Atlantic Ocean all the year round. Some are huge vessels, well-appointed and well-manned; others are small craft that seem scarcely fit for so vast a voyage, for it is three thousand miles, more or less, according to the port of departure, and the passage always uncertain, and often stormy. Compared with much longer voyages—that to Australia, for example—the perils of crossing the Atlantic are far greater. The sailor can never count on the wind and weather two days together, as in the seas where the steady trade-winds blow.

Not to go back to the ancient Norsemen, who were the first, it is now generally believed, to touch the coasts of North America, the voyage of Christopher Columbus is the earliest in authentic history. There are few boys who have not heard of the long delays and bitter disappointments which hindered the brave Genoese from attempting to carry out the dreams of his early life. It was not till he was fifty-six years of age that he obtained the patronage of King Ferdinand and Queen Isabella of Spain, and persuaded Martin Alonzo Pinzon, a wealthy navigator, to supply the ships and funds for the expedition. At last the little squadron of three vessels sailed from Palos, a poor trading-port on the coast of Andalusia, on Friday, August 3rd, 1492.

So solemn and terrible an undertaking it seemed to cross the ocean, beyond which Columbus felt sure there was another world unknown to the ancients, that he went publicly to confession and communion, and would no doubt have made his will if he had had any property to leave. But even his small share of the expense was advanced to him on the faith of his sanguine promises.

We are not going to tell anything now of his romantic adventures, but wish to notice chiefly the small size of the vessels. Only one, the "Santa Maria," prepared expressly for the expedition, was decked. On this the admiral hoisted his flag. The other two were light barques, called caravels, not larger than our coasting or deep-sea fishing boats, without deck in the centre, but built high at prow and stern, with forecastle and cabins for the crew.

The "Pinta" was commanded by Martin Pinzon, with his brother Francisco as pilot. Another brother, Vicente Pinzon, commanded the "Niña," a single-masted boat with lateen sails. In the three boats there were 120 persons, all told, ninety of them seamen, the others including notaries, physicians, servants, and private adventurers or traders.

It was on the 25th of September, the fifty-second day of the voyage, that the joyous cry of "Land!" was heard, and all joined in chanting the "Gloria in excelsis." It was a false alarm, however, and not till Friday, the 12th of October, did they set foot on *terra firma*. For many days the dejection of the voyagers was as great as had been their sudden elation.

Columbus alone sustained his hope amidst the gloom and the despair of all. By steering ever to the west he knew he must come to India, or to Cipango of the East (Japan), if he found no land intervening. And he came upon the islands of the West Indies just in time to be saved from the violence of the now mutinous crews. This spirit they showed even after land-birds had come to the ships, and herbage, fresh and green, was floating by. Terror and superstition prevailed, and these hopeful signs were regarded as so many delusions luring them to destruction. But all ended well, and the three ships of Columbus are named with immortal honour.

But now let us come home to our own time, and see three other vessels, crossing the Atlantic from the West towards Europe. It is no voyage of mysterious terror and untried adventure with these modern voyagers. Three trim pleasure yachts, such as we see on our own waters, are careering across the ocean on a racing match. It is an event worth briefly recalling in contrast to the old voyage of the caravels of Columbus.

In 1851 the arrival of the far-famed yacht "America" had caused a great sensation among yachting men, and no little astonishment was expressed when she carried off the prize in all the matches of the season at Ryde. It was plain that something was to be learned from the other side of the Atlantic.

In 1866 the great "ocean yacht race" came as a new surprise. Three vessels contested this race, the "Henrietta," the "Fleetwing," and the "Vesta," the two former being regular schooner-built keel boats, and the latter what is called a centre-board vessel—that is, fitted with a shifting keel, which could be drawn up at pleasure—a great advantage when sailing before the wind with a light breeze, but not so safe in a rough sea, with foul or head wind.

The "Henrietta" carried twenty-two seamen, besides her sailing-master, several experienced navigators, and her owner, Mr. Bennett, of the *New York Herald*, twenty-eight souls all told. The "Fleetwing" and the "Vesta" had each twenty-two on board.

The race was not for honour only, but a

The Great Ocean Yacht race, 1866.

sweep of 30,000 dollars each was entered into, the winner to pocket the whole, making a gain of somewhere about 10,000*l.*

The course was from Sandy Hook bar to Cowes, no time allowance, and the first arrived to win.

They started December 11th, 1866, at one o'clock, the sun shining brightly, with blue sky, but the air keen and frosty. An immense flotilla of steamers, yachts, boats, and all manner of craft went down the bay to see them off, with universal huzzahing and with playing of the "Star-spangled Banner" and "Yankee Doodle."

The "Henrietta" ran 235 miles in the first twenty-four hours from the start, after which she averaged fourteen knots an hour throughout the voyage. She encountered very heavy weather half way across, having several men washed overboard, and having to lay to some hours. She kept on the same tack all through, hardly veering ten miles from a straight line drawn on the chart from Sandy Hook till she sighted the Needles. Passing this point on the afternoon of Christmas Day, she reached Cowes the same evening, completing the voyage from Sandy Hook in 13 days, 22 hours, 46 minutes. The "Fleetwing" came in one hour and twenty minutes later, and the "Vesta" at four next morning, so that it was a very close run over a distance of more than 3000 miles.

There was nothing wonderful in this race, which proved the excellence of the boats, but gave no opportunity for much skill in seamanship. An English yacht, the "Themis," had not long before crossed, and gone down the coast, and through the Straits of Magellan. Lord Dufferin had also made his adventurous voyage in "High Latitudes" in a yacht less than half the size of the "Henrietta."

The ocean feats of the caravels of the

fifteenth century or the yachts of our own time have been surpassed by daring voyagers who have crossed the Atlantic in far smaller vessels.

One of the most remarkable instances was the voyage of Captain Thomas Crapo and his wife, in a boat called the "New Bedford," so named after the port of New Bedford, Massachusetts, from which they sailed. It was a boat of about two tons' burden, with two masts, and was schooner-rigged, with what are called leg-of-mutton sails. Leaving New Bedford on the 28th May, 1877, and Chatham (Massachusetts) on the 2nd June, the Wolf Rock Light, off Land's End, Cornwall, was sighted on the 22nd July, and anchor cast off Newland, Penzance, the same night at eleven. The captain was an experienced sailor, having already crossed the Atlantic twenty-one times. The passage, though on the whole uneventful, was sometimes very rough, and we admire the pluck and skill of Captain Crapo and the endurance of his wife, who would not let him go without her. She was said to be a native of Glasgow, but her father a Swede, and her mother a native of Newcastle-on-Tyne.

Captain Crapo's voyage beat all that had gone before as to the size of his boat, but a more remarkable passage has been since made by the two brothers Andrews, of Boston, in the "Nautilus," by far the smallest boat that has ever crossed the Atlantic. In length it is under twenty feet, in breadth about six and a half, in depth two feet three inches.

This tiny shell of a boat was at the Paris Exhibition, and was afterwards seen in London and at Brighton, where the editor of *The Boy's Own Paper* made the acquaintance of the adventurous brothers, and arranged for publishing a narrative of the voyage.

CHAPTER III.

Perils of the Atlantic.

Although old voyagers speak unconcernedly about the broad Atlantic as an "Ocean Ferry," large steamers perpetually going to and fro, and although the passage is usually safe with good ships and good seamanship, yet it is liable to many of "the dangers of the deep."

In the old times, when only sailing ships were known, never a year passed without a sad list of wrecks and disasters. So terrible were the losses, that the British Admiralty set on foot official inquiries as to the cause of the frequent storms on certain parts of the Atlantic. The result of the inquiry was that the uncertain and violent winds are chiefly caused by the irregularity between the temperature of the Gulf Stream and of the regions reached by it.

The Gulf Stream is the name given to a great body of water ever flowing northward from the equator towards the poles, in certain well-defined parts of the ocean. It is this stream which carries the temperature of summer, even in the dead of winter, as far north as the Grand Banks of Newfoundland. The moisture deposited from the warmer air, on reaching colder atmosphere, is the cause of the fogs that commonly cloud that region.

The usual dampness of the British Islands, especially of Ireland, is due to this great ocean stream, which has at the same time the beneficent effect of tempering the cold of winter in north-western Europe. But for its influence the climate of Britain would be as rigorous as that of the coasts of Labrador, which are ever fast-bound in fetters of ice, though in the same latitude. Sometimes the harbour of St. John's, Newfoundland, has been closed with ice as late as the month of June; yet who ever heard of the port of Liverpool, on the other side, though two degrees farther north, being closed with ice even in winter?

But while the Gulf Stream has this benign influence on the climate of Europe, it has often a disastrous effect on the atmosphere of the ocean. Captain Maury, to whom science owes much of its knowledge of ocean currents, says that "the Gulf Stream is, to use a sailor expression, the great weather-breeder" of the North Atlantic Ocean. The most furious gales sweep along with it; and the dense fogs of the north, which so much endanger navigation in winter, doubtless owe their existence to the presence, in that cold sea, of immense volumes of warm water brought by the Gulf Stream.

Sir Philip Brooke found the air on each side of it at the freezing point, while that of its waters was 80° of Fahrenheit. The heavy, warm, damp air over the current caused great irregularity in his chronometers. The excess of heat daily brought northward by the waters from the tropics would, if suddenly set free, be sufficient to make the column of superincumbent atmosphere hotter than molten iron. With such an element of atmospherical disturbance in its bosom, we might expect storms of the most violent kind to accompany it in its course. Accordingly, the most terrific that rage on the ocean have been known to be near its borders. Some of these great storms begin far away in the tropics, and travel northwards as cyclones, their force not always being spent before reaching the shores of western Europe.

These are the disturbances, the existence and passage of which are now regularly telegraphed from America, and of which due notice appears in the weather-warnings of the meteorological tables published in our daily papers. But apart from these great hurricanes, some of which have left dark records in history, there are constant disturbances caused by the varying temperature of the ocean, rendering the weather of the Northern Atlantic always changeable and uncertain.

Since the introduction of steam navigation the dangers of the Atlantic have been greatly lessened, although disasters when they do occur are of a magnitude unknown before. The first steamer that crossed the Atlantic was the "Sirius," in 1838, the year after the accession of Queen Victoria. In the year 1841 the first great disaster occurred, in the mysterious and still unexplained disappearance of the "President." The latest account we have of her is that she left New York on the 11th of March, having on board, among many passengers, a son of the Duke of Richmond, the Rev. B. Cookman, and Mr. Power, a popular author and actor of Irish characters. Whether the ill-fated vessel was overwhelmed in a tempest, like the "Cambria" in 1870, or caught fire like the "Amazon" in 1852, or was run down by another vessel like the "Ville de Havre" in 1873, will never now be known. As icebergs are rarely met with in the course she would have taken, this could hardly have been the cause of her doom, although sometimes a real source of danger.

We read, for instance, in the month of April of this year, that on her way to New York the Belgian steamer "Ferdinand Van der Taelan," Captain Catloor, was laid to on the night of the 18th ult., owing to the presence of ice in the Atlantic. At daybreak, the weather being clear and very cold, a tremendous iceberg was observed towering over the deck of the steamer. Measurements taken by means of the sextant showed the height of the berg to be 300 ft., its length about 1000 ft., and its thickness 400 ft. In view of the danger of continuing on her course the steamer's head was turned to the southward, and the ice was left behind. A heavy gale was met on the 20th, and on the 23rd a wooden vessel about 70 ft. long was passed floating bottom up.

It is a terrible fact, which may startle some of our readers, that in thirty years after the loss of the "President" nearly sixty steamers, including the West India mail-boats, have been destroyed while on their passage across the Atlantic. Of these, seven, after leaving port, disappeared and have never since been heard of. Four were run down by or "collided" with other vessels. Four were burned. One, the "Canadian," ran on sunken ice in the Straits of Belle Isle on the 4th June, 1861; one, the "Helena Sloman," foundered in mid ocean in November, 1850; and another, the " Hibernia," met the same fate off the coast of Ireland in 1868.

The remainder of the melancholy list, or about one each year, were wrecked either on the Irish or British coasts, or on those of America, or on islands and rocks off them. One only, the " Iowa," an American vessel, was wrecked on the French coast, near Cherbourg, in 1864. At least eight of the sixty ran on the shores of either Nova Scotia or Newfoundland, in the foggy weather which usually endangers these regions.

There has been a proportional number of losses in the last few years, but we have not the detailed report of recent wrecks before us. One fearful and hitherto undescribed cause of disaster was revealed by the discovery of what can be only called an infernal plot by a German to destroy an emigrant steamer, by causing an explosion of dynamite during the passage. A piece of skilful mechanism was arranged so as to sink the ship with all souls on board, for the sake of the insurance money upon part of the cargo. The providential explosion of the charge prematurely, before starting, led to the discovery of the nefarious plot, and has caused the uncomfortable suspicion that some of the previous mysterious losses may possibly have been due to similar causes.

On the 12th of November, 1879, the Guion Steamship Company's new liner, the "Arizona," carrying nearly four hundred human beings and a valuable cargo, came into violent collision with an iceberg, owing to its vicinity not having been discovered in time. It appears that at about eight o'clock on the evening of the day in question, a heavy black cloud arose across the "Arizona's" bows, increasing in density during the next three-quarters of an hour. The vessel was going at full speed, and it was with the greatest difficulty that the men on the look-out could make out objects immediately ahead.

The "whale-back," as it is called, or covered roof at the extreme point of the bows, to prevent the noble craft from shipping water when she dips her nose into a wave, was in course of being painted, and therefore the look-outs, instead of taking their customary places upon the " whale-back," were relegated to the " skid bridge " just behind it. The Liverpool stipendiary magistrate, assisted by three competent and experienced sea-captains as assessors, have pronounced the decision of the Court of Inquiry instituted by the Board of trade with a view to investigating the circumstances of the accident, which happily resulted in no loss of life, but which might in an instant have plunged four hundred souls into the whirlpool of waters.

It transpired before the Court of Inquiry, that on the day before her encounter with an iceberg, the "Arizona" passed—fortunately by daylight—an abandoned vessel so closely that her sailors and passengers could, without difficulty, read the ship's name, and the port of Sunderland, upon the derelict's bows. The incident recalls a danger from which, especially by night, vessels ploughing the great deep can never hope to be free.

Mr. Thomas Brassey has more than once expressed the opinion that deserted vessels of this kind are almost as formidable to their living sisters as a sunken rock. In the "Voyage in the 'Sunbeam'" it is recorded that one morning her master and owner went on deck, when some 350 miles west of Ushant, and that about half-past ten a cry of "Sail on the port beam!" caused general excitement on board the "Sunbeam." Every telescope in the yacht was brought to bear upon the stranger, and orders were given to steer direct for the vessel. "Soon we were near enough," says the narrative, "to send a boat's crew on board, while we watched their movements anxiously from the bridge. She was from two to three hundred tons' burden, and beneath her white bowsprit the gaudy image of a woman served as figure-head. We could now read her name—the 'Carolina'—surmounted by a gorgeous yellow decoration on her stern." The "Carolina" was a derelict, with her masts snapped off close to the deck and her bulwarks gone. She was laden with port wine and cork, and it was with difficulty that the crew could be restrained from bringing some of the wine on board the "Sunbeam." To have towed the deserted vessel into the nearest port—nearly 400 miles distant—would have been too long a job, nor, with the limited appliances on board the "Sunbeam," was it possible to blow the "Carolina" up; "and thus," says Mrs. Brassey, "we were obliged to leave her floating about as a derelict, a fertile source of danger to all ships crossing her track."

With her buoyant cargo, and the trade winds slowly wafting her to smoother seas, it may probably be some years before she breaks up. Who can say whether, at this moment, the hapless "Carolina" may not be still afloat and full of menace to some "good tall ship" which may have the ill-luck to run into her? The incident shows the often unconsidered dangers to which vessels at sea are perpetually exposed.

By those who have not closely studied the subject, it is generally supposed that shipwrecks are mostly caused by the raging of the elements. This is certainly the chief source of fear to landsmen in anticipation of a voyage. But of thirty vessels which went on shore, not more than three or four appear to have suffered directly in consequence of heavy weather. Miscalculation as to distances run, or courses steered, unreckoned currents of the ocean, clouded nights or foggy days, and the absence of strict watch, have been the chief causes of disaster. The want of discipline implied in the last-named cause has been at the bottom of many calamities, especially by fire, and by collision with other vessels. It is noteworthy that during the thirty-three years of which we have been speaking, the Cunard Company, on board whose liners the discipline is as strict as in Her Majesty's Navy, never had damage done to one ship, nor lost a man by the perils of the sea.

There is a weird fascination in reading the accounts of the terrible disasters that befall great steamships. Few of the sixty wrecks and calamities referred to but were attended with serious loss of life. When the "Atlantic" was wrecked on Meagher's Head, off Nova Scotia, in 1873, no less than 562 persons

The Cunard steamer "Scotia," the largest transatlantic paddle-wheel boat.

were drowned; with the "City of Glasgow," in 1854, 480 people perished. When the "Austria" was burned in mid-ocean, in 1858, 470 lives were lost; with the "Arctic," 300; with the "Anglo-Saxon," 372; and with the "Ville de Havre," when struck by the "Lochearn," in 1873, 226 went down. That year was fatal to no less than six great steamers, but the average of the whole period for 1838 to 1878, has not been above three ships in every two years.

Of all these disasters, the one which produced the greatest impression of horror was the loss of the "Amazon," West India Mail steamer, by fire, in 1852. She was the largest steamship ever then launched from an English dockyard. Her officers and crew numbered 110 men, and she carried fifty passengers, among whom was the lamented Eliot Warburton, author of the popular book of travels, "The Crescent and the Cross."

She left Southampton January 2nd. The engines were soon found to work badly, and heated the surrounding woodwork, much of which was Dantzic pine, a most inflammable material. She had not been thirty-six hours at sea when, as she was entering the Bay of Biscay against a strong head-wind, flames suddenly burst forth from the engine-room. All efforts to subdue them proved unavailing. There were boats enough to carry all on board, but through difficulty in lowering them, as too commonly happens, only two boats, the pinnace and dingy, got afloat, and saved 58 out of the 162 who left England, the other boats being capsized or burned.

After giving this saddening account of disasters, it is only right to turn to the brighter side of the record. Let it be remembered that now on an average there is a steamer starting from an American or European port every day in every year. Thus, after all, the percentage of losses is not great, and the risks of life are really not greater by sea than by land, even when the voyage is across the Atlantic. Then it is certain that the disasters are fewest where the ships are well-built and well-manned, and where discipline is best kept up. The prosperous career of the Cunard ships we have already noted, and there are now few mishaps to the ships of the other great Companies who share the passenger traffic.

Accidents at sea never happen without a cause, and in rare instances is a tempest or other natural or external influence the cause of disaster. Mr W. H. Kingston, a good authority in nautical matters, and well acquainted with the history of transatlantic voyages, has thus written: "It may be affirmed that if steamers are properly built, their machinery thoroughly strong and sound, if their cargo is well-stowed, if due precautions are taken against fire, if they are carefully navigated, and a vigilant look-out kept in fine weather as well as foul, there is the least possible risk from the dangers of the sea. The passage across the Atlantic should be as safe as that between England and Ireland, and safer than a journey from London to Edinburgh."

The perils against which it is least easy to take precaution are those caused by ice or by floating wreckage. To avoid the former it is usual for steamers to take as far southward a course as possible at the season when ice is likely to be met with. The floating wreckage can only be avoided by perpetual watchfulness in the look-out.

We have given these particulars about ocean navigation, both because the subject is interesting in itself, and because many readers will sometime cross the Atlantic in steamers, or in sailing ships.

Floating wreckage on the Atlantic.

CHAPTER IV.

Perils of the "Nautilus" and Crew.

The voyage of these two Americans in their little "Nautilus," implied perils tenfold more serious than the passage of any steamer or sailing vessel. Besides the dangers from winds and waves, or from being run down in fog or darkness, a small craft is more liable to injury from floating spars or other drifting wreckage always abounding in the Atlantic. But far more perilous was the risk from the long exposure and the continuous strain, with prospect of little rest and less sleep. The odds were greatly against the success of the adventure, and this would be more decidedly the opinion, after the failure of an attempt made since, with very distressing and almost fatal results. In fact many old salts, even after seeing the boat and the men, retain a certain incredulity as to the voyage being fairly made all the way without any towing or other aid. The perusal of the log will alone suffice to remove all doubts, and to secure due honour to the brothers Andrews for their skill, pluck, and perseverance.

This honour was heartily accorded to them by the voice of public opinion, uttered through the press, both in England and France as well as America. As soon as the arrival in Europe, in Cornwall, could be heard of, special reporters and interviewers made their appearance, one of whom, the correspondent of the *New York Herald* in London, telegraphed back to America the substance of the log, from which he took extracts, descriptive of the voyage. The voyage was resumed, after a few days' rest, for Havre and for Paris, the great Exposition offering a tempting opportunity for introducing the "Nautilus" to the crowded Paris of 1878.[1] What was thought of the voyage may be seen from part of an article in the *Continental Gazette*, Paris, Sept. 5th, 1878:—

"Every American now in Paris, every American who admires pluck and daring,

---

[1] The French bill announcing the exhibition at Paris is a curiosity worth preserving. At the head is a picture of the boat with sail set.

L'INCROYABLE.
UNE
Traversée de l'Océan de Boston au Havre en 45 Jours,
SUR UNE COQUILLE DE NOIX.

Les deux frères ANDREW viennent d'accomplir la traversée la plus audacieuse jusqu'à ce jour à travers l'Océan sur un batelet appelé le NAUTILUS, dont les dimensions démontrent le courage de ces hardis navigateurs. Venez 6 bis, Avenue Rapp, vous faire expliquer par eux toutes les péripéties du voyage, voir le bateau et tous les accessoires qui ont servi à la traversée.

and who respects success, should pay a visit to the building near the Exposition in the Avenue Rapp, where two adventurous Yankees have installed the cockle-shell in which in forty-five days they crossed the stormy and capricious Atlantic.

"It is a wonderful example of human will conquering natural difficulties. There was everything to oppose these men in their enterprise. Surges sang dirges to them, but they would not listen. Monsters of the deep sniffed contemptuously at the little one-ton boat, and sometimes followed it as if they intended an attack. The winds blew and threatened. The rains descended and stiffened the limbs of the two bold men. But they sailed on. Each man took his turn at the helm for four hours at a time. The little craft was so often below the horizon that observations were taken with difficulty. Several times there were calms which almost brought despair to the hearts of the striving men. 'But,' says Walter, 'if it had not been for one of those calms, I should not have been here now. We had a chance to board the ship "C. L. Carney," of New York, and the captain gave me some Fryar's Balsam, which cured a grievous hemorrhage, which put my life in danger.'

"One can hardly believe that such a diminutive craft as the 'Nautilus' could stand the wear and tear of ocean travel as he gazes at her thin half-inch deck and sides. There is not room for a grown man to turn over in her little cabin. The Andrews brothers were compelled to keep their wet clothes on day after day, and their sleep was always broken. Sometimes they did not rest at all for a week. They had hot coffee but few times in the forty-five days, and they ate but little. They set their whole reserve force, and it appears to have been great, to the task of getting across. Such men deserve cordial recognition. They are not even sailors. They are artisans. They had their own lack of knowledge against them. But they have demonstrated what strong will can do. Go and see the 'Nautilus.' It is something which you will never forget."

The Paris *Figaro* was equally generous and enthusiastic in their praise. The *New York Herald* devoted two columns to the "Nautilus" and crew; also the London *Standard*, and other journals on both sides the Atlantic. The papers in fact were all very profuse with both illustrations and articles, and the brothers modestly said, "We unite in humbly thanking the press of the world for the courtesy that has been extended towards us."

Boston Harbour.

CHAPTER V.

Start of the "Nautilus" from Boston, and Log of the Voyage.

We must now recross to the American side, and go back to June 7th, 1878, when the "Nautilus" started from the harbour of Boston, Massachusetts. The following appeared in the *Boston Herald* of the following day, June 8th:—

"Departure of the Nautilus—the Andrews Brothers sail from City Point to cross the Atlantic in their little Boat—A good Start and much warm Encouragement.

"At three o'clock yesterday afternoon the very smallest boat that ever started to cross the Atlantic Ocean sailed from Mr. P. Coyne's Wharf, foot of O Street, City Point, bound for Paris, France. For several weeks the two Andrews Brothers, who take this little boat across, have been busily engaged preparing for the trip. They intended to start last Tuesday, but, owing to a dead east wind, they delayed till yesterday, which fortunately turned out to be a splendid day, and just such a one as they had been wishing for. A bulletin on the pier announced that the start would be made sharp at three p.m, but as early as eleven in the forenoon the stone pier was crowded, and the good-humoured throng waited patiently till the hour of sailing without murmuring. The several intervening hours were spent examining the boat and scanning the physique of the two men who were to attempt the hazardous undertaking of sailing her across the Atlantic.

"The boat was built at Gloucester, Mass.,

a short time ago, specially for this trip. She is a lap-streaked Dory. Her exact dimensions are 15 ft. on the bottom, 19 ft. over all, 6 ft. 7 in. wide, and 2 ft. 3 in. deep. She has only one short mast near the bow, making her something of a cat rig. When launched she looks a great deal smaller than she really is. She is decked over from stem to stern, with two small hatchways, one mid-ships and the other aft, where the helmsman sits and steers.

" She has one sail for ordinary weather—a lateen sail, which, when set, describes an acute triangle with the base resting on the deck of the boat. There is also a storm-sail, to be used when hove to at the drogue. They carry with them a Baker's improved oil compass, and an old-fashioned second-hand quadrant. They have a stock of provisions intended to last sixty days, mostly canned goods. They have sixty gallons of water in six ten-gallon kegs. As fast as the fresh water is consumed the kegs will be filled with salt-water.

"Should the two passengers of this little craft desire to have warm food, they can heat it with an oil stove or alcohol stove, both of which they have.

"For the purpose of heaving-to at sea, they are provided with a novel kind of anchor (the drogue). It is a large canvas barrel-shaped bag, attached to fifty fathoms of rope. During a storm this will be thrown into the water, and with their storm-sail set, and everything made snug, they can ride out a gale in mid-ocean. The boat is painted white, with a red, white, and blue stripe along her gunwale.

"The men who intend to sail across the Atlantic Ocean in the 'Nautilus' are brothers. The older, Wm. A. Andrews, is thirty-five years of age, was born in Manchester, Mass., and has had only a small amount of real experience as a sailor. The report that they

William A. Andrews.

Asa Walter Andrews.

were sailors from boyhood is erroneous. William once visited the Grand Banks as a fisherman, and that is the sum total of his experience in navigation. He is married—has a wife and three children. They saw him off yesterday, and will remain here till they hear from him. A. Walter Andrews, aged twenty-three years, is unmarried, was born in Beverly, Mass., at which town both young men were reared. Walter has been to the Grand Banks several times as a fisherman, and has an inborn love for the sea. He has had several narrow escapes from drowning.

"The start, that had been announced for Friday, naturally drew an immense throng of people, who crowded about the piers, piazzas, and roof of Mr. P. Coyne's hotel. Both sexes and all ages were represented. The bay was alive with craft—yachts, rowboats, and sculls from the rowing-club houses. Dories skimmed hither and thither. Several steam yachts kept up a constant whistling and puffing, adding a great deal of commotion to the scene.

"At ten minutes to three o'clock, while a light breeze was fanning up from the westward, the "Nautilus," with her snow-white lateen sail fully set, gracefully tacked away from the floating stage to which she had been moored, and dropped leisurely out into the bay, about fifty yards from the shore, and then paused for about ten minutes.

"At her peak were the Stars and Stripes of the United States and the Tricolour of France. The two flags snapped out loudly as they flashed in the wind. Walter Andrews sat smilingly at the helm; standing in front of him, and peering vaguely towards the east, was William, over whose face was a clearly defined expression of anxiety. As he stood there he seemed to be measuring the magnitude of the dangers that he had to face. On the boat sat Dr. Deering and his sister, friends of the brothers Andrews.

"Sharp at three o'clock, three loud cheers rang out from the throngs along the piers, and the little boat started eastward on her perilous journey. As she passed through the flotilla of yachts that were sailing about the bay, she received many cheers. The yacht 'Hermes' was the first to salute the 'Nautilus' with a gun. Salutes were then fired in the following order by the following yachts:—'Enterprise,' 'Wivern,' 'Gracie,' and 'Ivy,' the latter following up until opposite Long Island Light, and then gave the parting salute. The steamer 'Governor Andrew,' the 'Three Brothers,' the Shawmut Boat Club steamer, and many others, honoured the tiny boat with salutes. The yachts, 'Gracie,' 'Louella,' 'Brenda,' 'Prima Donna,' 'White Swallow,' 'Mist,' and a number of smaller craft, followed the young adventurers far out beyond Long Island Light. Here Dr. Deering and sister bade farewell to their friends, the Andrews Brothers, and got on board of the 'Prima Donna,' and returned to City Point, while the 'Nautilus' kept eastward on her course, until she faded out of sight. After she had disappeared, at five o'clock a stiff west wind blew up.

" They will make Land's End, England, first, and then proceed to Havre, France."

So much for the "Boston Herald's" narrative, which mentions various things better told by another than by the heroic voyagers. And now to the

LOG OF THE "NAUTILUS."

Friday, June 7th, 1878.—Left Captain Coyne's Wharf, City Point, South Boston, Massachusetts, for Havre, France, at three o'clock this p.m., amid an enthusiastic send-off. When off Long Island wind shifted to east. Was advised to go to Beverly, and take the next fair wind from there; so we parted company of friends. But the wind soon came round to S.W., and we bore away on our course. Yacht "Violet" spoke us off Boston Light, bidding us "God speed." Soon after tug-boat "Camilla" overhauled and spoke us. Soon left Minots Light out of sight, and shortly after sighted Highland Light, Cape Cod. The wind blowing a gale, the top of our binnacle came off, and went overboard. Shortly our white light lantern, our only light except the binnacle, went out by the pitching of the boat. Shortly after, the globe cracked and the side fell out. Soon our small binnacle light burnt out dry, leaving us in total darkness. Walter had to turn out and fill it in the dark as best he could, our little craft pitching heavily. Shortly after something very serious happened, and then we concluded to return and repair damages, to make our berth a little more convenient, and get more substantial lights. When we put about, Highland Light bore S.W., distant about twelve miles, and was visible at daylight; also the Highlands. We saw a shoal of whales this morning off Cape Cod, spouting and playing around us, also some porpoises.

Saturday, June 8th.—Wind S.W. Sighted Minots Lighthouse, and bore away for Beverly. Took observation as best I could with cloudy sky and bad horizon; four miles E. of Boston Lighthouse, and made my latitude 42.20 N. I did not try to get longitude. Arrived in Beverly at 4 p.m. After fixing toilet and eating a few baked beans, left there at 5.48 for Boston. Arrived home at 8.30 p.m., creating considerable excitement, my wife asking where was Walter, &c. I felt terribly mortified at losing such a good

A shoal of Porpoises.

chance to get off the coast, and wondered how folks would talk about our returning, &c. But let them wonder; we know ourselves what we are doing. Every small boat has put in somewhere before leaving the land for good.

I felt terribly stiff and sore all over, and went right to bed to get rested; did not want to see anybody. But I did allow my old friend Abbott an interview. Of course the remark was made that the old saying of sailing on Friday worked true enough, in our case any way. It commenced to rain at 4 p.m., and drizzled all night. Made up my mind that it was all for the best.

Sunday, June 9th.—The arrival of the "Nautilus" at Beverly was announced in the Beverly "Herald." There was a wrong statement in regard to our compass, it saying the needle broke, which was not the case. Wind N.; rainy at intervals.

Monday, June 10*th.*—Wind N.E. Rainy at intervals.

Tuesday, June 11*th.*—Wind N.E. Crowds flock from far and near to see the " Nautilus," the little beauty, as she lies moored in the dock.

Wednesday, June 12*th.*—Wind S.W. Took our departure from Beverly. Wind changed to S.E. Course E. by S. Had a good escort of Beverly friends as far as Baker's Island. Got poor observation, latitude 42.33 N.; wind E., then N.E., then S.E.; the wind very light; course various. Spoke " Lapstreak " boat, Captain Warren Jaquith. He told us not to carry sail too long on the " Nautilus." Thunder and lightning with some rain at 8 p.m. Calm from 9 p.m. till daylight. Lost sight of Thatcher's Island Light at 2 a.m. Run about thirty miles.

Thursday, June 13*th.*—Light westerly winds. Several sails in sight. Coffee for breakfast. Saw one whale and few porpoises. Got observation, latitude 42.14 N. Plenty of mackerel and mackerel sharks. Becalmed almost all day and all night. We have drifted nearly twenty miles off our course to the southward and eastward, making a run of about thirty miles.

Friday, June 14*th.*—Foggy and calm. Fog lifted at 11 a.m. Saw three sails in sight. Got out our oars and started a fine white ash breeze, and spoke one of them, the British schooner "Jennie T. Hibbard," Captain W. H. Dean, latitude 42.22 N., longitude 69.37 W. Being no wind the captain prevailed on us to come on board and get some dinner and recreation. It seems as though we had been out a week on the voyage. At 5 p.m., a light wind springing up, we left him, wishing us good luck, &c. Wind increased, and blew good breeze all night. The "Nautilus" behaved splendidly; course E. by

S. half S.; wind S.E.; changed to S.W. Run fifty-five miles. Fog came on at 10 p.m., and remained all night.

Saturday, June 15th.—Morning foggy and cold; wind S.W. During a gleam of the fog saw a schooner. She saw us and ran down and spoke us. Proved to be the "Commonwealth," of Gloucester, a mackerel-catcher, 117 miles from Thatcher's Island. Got observation, latitude 42.17 N. Soon set in foggy. Passed many logs, planks, &c. Blew fog-horn occasionally; sometimes with response. Night very foggy. This keeping your eyes on the compass and watching for lights, blowing fog-horn, wet and cold without relief, watching the seas as they follow you, thinking now and again that you may hear a log come crashing through your half-inch cedar, is a novelty not to be desired long. We passed to the northward of "George's Stormy Banks" in the night. Course E. by S. half S. Run 100 miles.

Sunday, June 16*th.*—Walter made some royal coffee for breakfast. Wind S.W. by S. Had a good wash. Saw a ship and schooner to the southward. Sun out and fog disappearing. Feel better. Got observation, lat. 42.21 N. While getting observation was surrounded by shoal of porpoises, some striking the "Nautilus" with their tails. Two sails ahead. Passed Cunard steamer, distance one mile; at same time spoke fishing schooner "Triumph," of North Haven, Maine. Got a pair of mittens from her; gave them a corned shoulder "that we got from schooner, 'J. T. Hibbard' to grease our foretack with." Passed Brown's Bank. Big tide rips. Saw some very small birds resting on the water; saw one that could not fly; tried to catch him, but he dived under the "Nautilus." Moon rose awfully red. Passed a barque bound to

F

the westward. Course E.S.E. Run sixty-five miles.

Monday, June 17th.—Sun rose very red; wind S.W., light. Latitude by observation 42.13 N. Course E. by S. half S. Saw no sails to-day. Saw one shark ahead and tried to run over him. Wind shifted to N.E. this evening; signs of a storm. " Beware of Sable Island." Thick fog set in. This is one of the luxuries in this part of " the Big Drink." Run about sixty-five miles.

Tuesday, June 18th.—Rainy and foggy. Wind S.E. No coffee to-day; no sails either. We are " monarchs of all we survey." "What are the wild waves saying, dear sister?" One wave broke clean over our little " Nautilus," but did not wet our bed, as Walter was in there, and the lid shut down. The sun came out for a few moments at about noon; tried to get observation, but it was imperfect. Latitude 42.14 N.; run fifty-five miles; wind shifted in the evening to S., then S.W. Cleared off and came on thick again. And it was so dark—oh! how dark!—you could not distinguish the water from the mist.

Wednesday, June 19*th.*—Wind S.W. ; bids fair to-day. " Coffee and sardines for two." Had a wash for a change. I saw a big smoke, and made for it; they saw us, and changed their course accordingly. She proved to be the White Star steamer " Adriatic," lat. 42.35 N., long. 59.20 W. Some one wanted to know if there were any more Yankees left over there. The purser wished to know if we wanted any fresh cooked stuff. Answered in the negative. She was from Liverpool, England, to New York. Could not hear anything scarcely for noise of steam blowing off. They gave us three rousing cheers, which we heartily reciprocated; and as we bore away for Havre they cautioned us to beware of the propeller. They had read of us in the English papers, the departure from Boston having been telegraphed. This made us feel "better than turkey and plum-pudding." More than 440 miles from home, saw another sail ahead; did not want to speak her. One was enough for to-day. She passed to windward of us. Got observation, lat. 42.30. Passed another ship, bound N.W. Wind S. and S.W. At 7.30 p.m. sighted another steamer. Run sixty miles.

Thursday, June 20th.—Wind S. and S.W., variable. A very heavy sea commenced running at 3 a.m.; had to reef, and shortly after to heave to. About 12 noon resumed our trip. Passed one of our namesakes, a nautilus, a fine specimen nine inches long. Passed two ships to leeward. About 2 a.m. heard horns blowing; saw green light, and spoke fine ship " Henrietta," from Newport to St. John's, New Brunswick. Blowing strong, and seas heavy. Could not say or talk much, it was so rough ; I do not think they saw anything but our light, for the captain wanted to know what schooner this was. We ex-

plained a little, and I know he was relieved, when he said he would report us. Wind N.E., course E. by S. Tried our square sail to-day ; did not amount to much, for it would not give us steerage-way. Run fifty miles.

We are in the gulf stream, and it must be a good degree to the northward of where it is laid down on the chart.

Saturday, June 21st.—Wind E. and N.E. Strong heavy sea running. Had to heave to and put out the drogue.[1] Soon took in the drogue and tried to run double-reefed. Could not. Tried our square sail, gave it up, and tried the drogue again. It looked like a storm in winter. The water was very bad from 3 p.m. till 2 a.m., 22nd. I don't want to see anything any worse while in the "Nautilus." Rain, fog, wind, and cold. No warm grub. I don't think I ever saw such seas before, nearly all of them breaking. We had to put all of our cable on to the drogue, unship the rudder, make everything snug. The waves were

---

[1] The drogue, as explained on p. 50, is a canvas cylindrical sack pendent from a broad hoop like the section of a barrel. When put out it steadies the boat, serving the purpose of a floating anchor. The drogue, it will be seen, was often in good use throughout the voyage.

"mountains," truly. Run and course very doubtful.

Saturday, June 22nd.—Lat. 42.53 N., long. 56.55 W. Just passed a "Portuguese man-of-war." Wind N.E. Came on foggy shortly

Portuguese Man-o'-War.

after sunrise; cleared up about 11 a.m. Very pleasant now. Picked up a bottle half-full of some sort of poor rum. Sunset very yellow, betokening plenty of wind to-morrow. The sea is bad enough now. Saw some skipjacks and stormy petrel. The plot thickens. Course S.E. Fog came on, but cleared soon after. Wind E. and E. by N. More nautili; water rough and head beat sea.

At 4 a.m., 23rd, Walter sighted green light ahead; gave one blast of fog-horn to let them know that we were on the starboard tack; proved to be a ship; showed our light, then put it out of sight and ran down to speak them; but the moment we doused the "glim" (our light) they turned and ran before it, and we after them, for a mile or so, but finding a stern chase a long one, we gave it up and let them go; so I blew my fog-horn and whistle alternately for a minute, and resumed our course as best we could on an E.S.E. wind. Shortly after they hove to till daylight. Whether they knew what we were or not I can't tell, but it is my impression that they must have taken us for the Flying Dutchman, and they did not want any of our correspondence. We are getting to be a terror in these waters; five days now banging around, hove to, and otherwise of no advantage to ourselves or any one else. Run and course under the circumstances very doubtful.

Mother Carey's Chickens.

Sunday, June 23rd.—Wind N.E. and E. and S.E., all easterly. Lat. 42.50. No longitude for me; foggy and discouraging enough. Got a rap on the head with the club of the sail, which nearly stunned me.

Coffee for breakfeast; tomatoes and ham for dinner. At 5 p.m. sighted a ship, and as the wind was E. by S., and we could not lie our course, we waited for him to come up. Proved to be the ship "Tyro," of Yarmouth, N.S., Captain Raymond, long. 55.20 W. Wanted to know if we wanted him to take us off. Told him we guessed not. There were some lady passengers on board; they cheered us heartily. Said his barometer indicated easterly winds; said he would report us. Shortly after concluded that it would not pay for wear and tear, so we hove to at drogue, and remained all night. We are on the edge of the gulf stream. Run and course of no consequence.

Monday, June 24th.—Wind S.E. and very high. Rough sea. Still at the drogue. Saw steamship bound to the eastward and two ships to westward. A terrible high combing sea running. Threw some oil to see what it was good for; found that the smell of the cod-liver oil was about as disagreeable as the clean water breaking over us. The smell summoned all the Mother Carey's chickens, hagdens, marble-headers, and other sea-birds, from far and near to us. What scent they have, and such a hurrah as they set up! Also a grampus came puffing along, and they were all disgusted, for they found only a "big cry and little wool." We are drifting to the N.W. Somehow or other, I can't keep Sable Island out of my mind, and I often stand up and look to leeward for it while at the drogue; also for sails.

Tuesday, June 25th.—Wind S.S.W. Bad sea running. Threw more oil. Don't mind the smell so much now, as the situation is becoming a little more interesting. Ah! can it be possible? Yes, it is true—the wind is moderating. We hauled the drogue in at 2 p.m., and started from this miserable place. Course S.E. by E. This is wild sailing. Oh, how I wish some of my chums could see old Bill now! Oh, that this scene could only be photographed on paper as it ever will be in my mind!

Came on foggy later in day. At dusk heard steam whistle. Blew our horn, showed our light, and saw a steamship coming head on. I gave the "Nautilus" a little starboard helm, and we passed within a few yards of her. I waved my hat; they cheered as they passed. I heard some one ask if they could do anything for us. I asked what steamer that was, and heard some one say "New York," and they were lost to view in the fog and dusk. I saw New York in letters on the starboard side of her round stern. She was travelling like the wind, and if she struck a vessel she would strike them hard. Well, I guess they knew their business. A Mother Carey's chicken flew into our sail, and was stunned and fell nearly dead into my lap. Oh, how I pitied the poor, quivering, fluttering visitor! I took it as a good omen, though, and, as it recovered (for all sea-birds cannot rise from any hard substance) I placed it out on the raging water again, and had the satisfaction of seeing it fly away in the darkness. Rain! Oh, how it rained! and how we flew! Sailed 200 miles these twenty-four hours.

Wednesday, June 26th.—Wind S.W. Passed near to a large barque, painted green, bound to the W. Have since learnt from a lady passenger who saw us that it was a Russian barque, and was lost soon after, all hands taking to a raft. They were bothered by whales, and wondered if the whales bothered us. Oh, how it rained this p.m. I think we drove the "Nautilus" twenty miles in two hours. Cleared off this evening. No observation to-day, or lately; it has been so rough and foggy. Passed a ship bound W. in the night; also a shoal of whales that were puffing, blustering, and "playing engine." Course S.E. by E. An old hagden sea-bird saw us, and thought he had made a discovery. He came up and whirled round us several times, but as we did not pan out well for him he left. Position doubtful.

Thursday, June 27th.—A heavy swell on this morning, but the first fine day for quite a spell. All that we have in the shape of clothes and bedding and everything else that is not air-tight are completely wet through. Stewed beans for breakfast. Course S.E. by E.; wind S.W. At night a shoal of whales kind of made us feel uncomfortable. You could touch some of them with your hand. Their blowing was terrific. I was turned in, and Walter called me. I got all ready to jump out of bed pretty quick. Feeling tired and sick, I lay down again, telling Walter if he saw any coming head on with their mouths open to call me. It was so dark you could not see twenty feet on the water. Some rubbed the boat with their sides. I think our light attracted them. There was but little wind, so we kept quiet, and believed in the old adage, that if you let them alone they will let you alone. I told Walter to put the light out of sight, which he did, but it made no difference. Shortly after I took the helm, and a breeze springing up, they departed, to our extreme pleasure. Early this morning a large steamer passed quite handy to us, but as they could not see us, kept right along. We wished that we had been a little farther that way. Feel better this morning, 28th. Calm, with little puffs from all quarters. Heavy swell running.

Friday, June 28th.—A royal breakfast—coffee with condensed milk, corned beef with "hard tack." Plenty of Mother Carey's chickens, hagdens, and marble-headers. Thick overhead. Had a good wash, and we are waiting for something to turn up. Walter has turned in for a short rest. Now he turns out we wedge our mast, make sail, and he turns in again. Got observation, though it was a hard job, 42.29 N., longitude, dead reckoning, 53.10 W. Passed between two ships, one going E. and the other W. This is the first one we have seen going E. Some whales. We did not show any light last night, just for fun.

Saturday, June 29th.—This morning at daybreak I felt terribly sleepy, and with the greatest difficulty I kept my post at the helm. In spite of my exertions, however, I could not refrain from a momentary drowse ; yet my previous experience as a soldier on guard often reminded me to be a man, and be as vigilant to my own cause as I was to that of my country. But in spite of my exertions I must have lost consciousness, for I was suddenly startled by hearing some voice halloaing to me, and looking up I expected to see some hardy Cape Ann fisherman attending to his trawls; but I was disappointed, for all I saw was fog and a deep heavy swell on the water, but I knew by the scene before me that I was on the southern edge of the Grand Banks of Newfoundland as well as if it had been a book with large letters, by a kind of inward instinct.

I was then reminded of my half-inch cedar boat, and about 100 fathoms of water between me and the most magnificent garden in the world. The bottom here was well portrayed by lines by Southey in his "Kehama," xvi. 5, which strangely came to my mind by way of contrast, I suppose:—

> "It was a garden still beyond all price—
> Even yet it was a place of Paradise.
>   *   *   *   *   *   *
> And here were coral-bowers,
> And grots of madrepores,
> And banks of sponge as soft and fair to eye
> As e'er was mossy bed

Whereon the wood-nymphs lie,
With languid limbs, in summer's sultry hours.
Here too were living flowers,
Which like a bud compacted,
Their purple cups contracted,
And now in open blossom spread,
Stretch'd, like green anthers, many a seeking head,
And arborets of jointed stone were there,
And plants of fibres fine as silkworm's thread,
Yea, beautiful as mermaid's golden hair
Upon the waves dispread.
Others that like the broad banana growing,
Raised their long wrinkled leaves of purple hue,
Like streamers wide outflowing."

But I am departing from my course, and such a contrast from the bottom of the sea to the top and our real condition! Occasionally I hear the well-known quack of what the sailors call hagdens, a sea-bird familiar hereabouts. I will to my dreary log again.

Wind N.W. for the first time since we started, course E.S.E., very light winds these last twenty-four hours. Did not sail over seventy-five miles. Rain, fog. Some whales.

Two ships so far away could not speak them. Running by dead reckoning now. Feel better than I expected, but not very well anyway. These last two weeks have been very hard on an old cripple like me. We hope for a better show now that we are up to the Grand Banks. When we see a ship the fog will shut her out, so we cannot get correct longitude, as we have no chronometer, and if we did it would be hard on the chronometer.

Sunday, June 30th.—Wind W., course E.S.E. Foggy. In the gulf stream to the southward of the Grand Banks, making our little five miles an hour now. Made a good 100 miles these last twenty-four hours. Made for two different ships to-day, but could not catch them. Baked beans for breakfast. Cleared up. Will write a letter and send it home by first vessel we can put it on board of.

This boat, I find, is awfully hard to steer in strong winds. She draws so little water, and is so round on the bottom. Only for our Baker's compass we would not be anywhere.

Wind increases. No observation to-day. Rain at intervals. Saw a fine ship behind us just after a shower; as she bore down we laid alongside and spoke her; proved to be the American ship "James H. Fish," of Thomaston, Maine, Captain Brown, bound to England. They got ready to pick us up, and were surprised when they found out that we were going farther than they were. Saw three women on board. Gave us his reckoning, and said he would report us. Latitude 43 N., longitude 47.16 W. Wind increased to a gale; had to reef.

Two hours after tried to put square sail on, but came near being swamped. Concluded to heave to at the drogue. Wind N.W.

We are drifting on our course. These are what Ralph Tomlinson calls "Cap Seas." Ralph Tomlinson is my brother-in-law. He told me that if we got by these seas, we should go over all right; but I took no notice of what he said till we got here. He is an Englishman, and has made many trips in a large steamer as engineer.

Monday, July 1st.—Got under way at 9 a.m. Saw five flying-fish. Walter caught a nautilus in our bucket, examined it, was disgusted, threw it away. Saw some rudder-fish. Lost my hat overboard, and got it again. Just as I was turning in this morning a sea boarded us, and about a barrel of water came into the bunk, completely saturating me and the bed. One sea swept our lantern overboard from its lashing behind the mast. We had to put it behind the mast to keep the wind and waves from putting it out. We are 100 miles east of southern edge of Grand Bank of Newfoundland. While heaving to last night, saw green light bearing down on to us. Hauled out our lantern to show a light, but it went out. Got the binnacle light, which is called a hurricane, and that went out too. Kept lighting them and passing them out one after the other several times. Finally the vessel passed a short distance from us at the rate of twelve knots an hour. Felt relieved somewhat. This is another of the luxuries of this kind of navigation.

Wind N.W. Got no observation, but more rain; just as well, perhaps. Wet, wet, everything wet. Drifted twenty miles up to 42 N.

Can it be possible? "Hand me the quadrant, quick, Walter, the sun is gleaming! Ah, I have him. Yes, I have. Latitude 43.10 N., longitude 46.30 W. How fortunate! Went sixty-six miles more. By this time the seas were running mountains high.

Tuesday, July 2nd.—Hove to at 6 a.m. Remained at drogue all day. Wind N.W., a gale, terrible tide, rips. More rain; fearful waves. During the day saw many Mother Carey's chickens dashed down on to the waves in a helpless condition. What a scene for a painter; but who could paint it?

A Swedish barkentine, named "Rudolph Gren," or something similar, passed near enough to speak to us. But we could not understand. They were going to heave to, but we beckoned to them to go along, which they did. Saw several vessels bound east and west. Rain and fog; cap seas. On edge of the stream. We allow one and a half miles an hour drift while at the drogue. I have given up trying to keep a real log, and make a mixture of log and memoranda.

As we are situated now we don't know "what moment will be our next," as Mrs. Parting- says.

Wednesday, July 3rd.—Wind N.N.W. Remained at drogue all day. Blowing a gale.

Saw several vessels bound E. and W. Rain and cold. No hot drinks to-day. Drifted about thirty miles up to 12 noon; am about used up. Lat. 43.10 N., long. 44.56 W., a fearful sea running.

> "A life on the ocean wave,"
>   The man who wrote it was green;
> He never had been to sea,
> And a storm he never had seen.

Thursday, July 4th.—Drank the bottle of lager that we had been saving for this occasion. Wind N.W. Lay at drogue all day. The most dangerous waves we have had to contend with yet. Towel washed overboard. Saw several sails going east.

Good day for them, poor day for us. No celebration for us but Nature's display of phosphorescent lights at night, much to our annoyance, often mistaking some of them for real lights for a few seconds. My mind was often on Boston Common. How strange the contrast! We place our lantern behind the mast, so that vessels going east and west can see it. Vessels from north cannot see it.

Friday, July 3th.—Hauled in the drogue at half-past 3 a.m. Wind W. Got under way. Wind shifted to S.W., then S., then S.E. Terrible chop sea. Came to drogue again at 12 noon. After two hours we hauled in the drogue again, wind N., and we drove her for twenty-five miles. When we lay down inside of this cockle-shell, and she is making time, which she does sometimes, you would think forty men were at work on the outside of her, and launching her at the same time. At night the wind was light to westward. More rain. The sun shines in Paris, I thought, and we shall see it there by-and-by.

Saturday, July 6th.—Wind nowhere. Up and down like Paddy's hurricane. After our toilet we saw barque ahead. Got out our oars, and soon had a fine ash breeze, and spoke Norwegian barque "M. Jollner," Captain Corneilinsen, from Gloucester to Baltimore, twenty-four days out, lat. 44 N., long. 42 W.; gave us three bottles of Allsopp's pale Indian ale, for use in sickness only. While eating dinner we were both taken awfully sick, and two bottles disappeared. More rain off and on. No observation. Wind S.W.; run under square sail all night. Storm brewing. During the day we made good time, almost burying the poor little "Nautilus" in the waves.

Sunday, July 7th.—Wind S.W. Blowing

a gale. Hove to at the drogue at daylight. The worst storm for us yet. One sea went three feet over my head while fixing the chaffing gear on the drogue line. More rain. Wind moderate in the evening, and

Sun-Fish (p. 92).

we put the square sail on. Run all night. At daylight put lateen sail on. When it is moderating after a storm, the waves slop over us worse than when it is blowing hard. Porpoises, skipjacks, Mother

Carey's, &c. Saw several sun-fish; never could make out what they were ever made for. I have been told their oil from the liver is highly beneficial for rheumatism.

Monday, July 8th.—Winds S. Spoke British ship "Republic," of Yarmouth, N.S., Captain Gold, bound to Antwerp, Belgium. Gave us half loaf of bread, half loaf of cake, and two dough-nuts; long. 36.30 W. Wind E. and S.E. Foggy; more rain. Shortly after spoke British ship "Khedive," of Hartlepool, bound to Boston. Gave lat. 45.05 N., long 37.50 W., a difference of only eighty miles in two hours. Remarks are unnecessary. Forgot to send my letter. It is a difficult thing to get near these ships without getting smashed when a heavy sea is running. Foggy, and more rain. Wind N.E. Saw steamship bound west. Eat cake and dough-nuts for breakfast, and soft bread for dinner. Puts me in mind of the Parker

House in war times. We are about half way across the ocean now, twenty-five days out. Everything has been against us, it seems. Oh! that we could have a pleasant day to dry some of this trash—for it is trash now.

Tuesday, July 9th.—Wind variable ahead. Foggy, and more rain. We hardly ever show a light in the night now unless we see one, and that is not very often. Run ninety miles. Course as close as we can lay it. No sails to-day.

Wednesday, July 10th. — Wind S.W.; foggy. More rain. No observation. Run 190 miles. That's getting up and getting on, for a small boat. Course E. by S. half S. Saw steamer and topsail schooner half-mile to leeward; run for them; could not head them off; blew horn to attract attention and show them some tall sailing, then bore away on our course.

Thursday, July 11th.—Wind W.; foggy. More rain for a change. For two hours Niagara Falls were discounted, a regular cataract of rain. Sun showed himself for a few minutes. Weather too ugly to try for an observation. Run 150 miles more. Making up now for lost time. Course E. by S. half S. No sails.

Friday, July 12th.—Wind S.; stormy; foggy. More rain, just to keep us cool and save washing ourselves. No observation. Course S.E. Run 190 miles. We usually heave to in weather like this, but we are anxious to get this job off our hands now. So we put the square sail on, and the wind working to the W., we drove her before it. Some of the waves would come over her stern and go the whole length of her, burying her completely; but she did nobly, and brought us out all right side up, with care. No sails.

Saturday, July 13*th.*—Foggy and misty; wind W. and N.W. Fog breaks away and sun comes out occasionally. Very cool. Ginger tea for breakfast. Rough water. Course E. by S. Spoke British barque "Martha," of Shoreham, bound to some creek in Nova Scotia. Long. 30 W. Got observation to-day, the first for eighteen days. Lat. 46.43. N. Pleasant in afternoon, which raises our spirits somewhat. Fog again at night, very thick. Run ninety miles. Course E. by S. half S.

Sunday, July 14*th.*—Foggy. Sun gleams occasionally. Opened one of our tin cans of hard bread. It is bully. Saw a fearful string of skipjacks jumping out of the water, and large fish similar to horse-mackerel, dolphins in chase, coming out five feet in the air, after them. They were getting their breakfast. Saw two sails. Wind N. Course E. by S. half S. Boston baked beans hot for dinner. Any quantity of porpoises, the wolves of the ocean. Lat., by observation, 46.51. N.; long. 28.10 W.; N. wind. Water smooth. We have only seen the moon several seconds for the first two quarters.

Monday, July 15th.—Wind E. and variable; smooth water. Spoke British brigantine "Maid of Llangollen," Captain Wellington Ring, of St. John's, N.B., from Port Madoc for St. John's, in ballast. Went on board, took dinner and lunch in afternoon. Lat. 47.10 N.; long. 28 W. Exchanged some of our grub for his; stretched our legs, and had a real good time generally. Sent my letter home; feel like a new man. Saw the moon several times in the night. When we had plenty of wind, we wanted it moderate; now we have it moderate, and we want more wind. Such is life. Can make no course. The fog bank in the eastern sky was black as ink, and dismal is no name for it. The "Nautilus" reminded me of the meeting of Philip Vanderdecken and his father, the captain of the phantom ship, for the last time before dissolution.

Tuesday, July 16*th.* — Wind E. and variable; very light. Saw five sails going to westward. Got observation. Lat. 46.49 N., long. 27.25 W. Get some wind in afternoon, but it shifts frequently, blowing in strong gusts. At midnight saw green light and shadow approaching off the starboard bow. Showed my light (which I keep under the seat now for two reasons—viz., we get the heat from it and can see more distinctly), and bore down on him, but he bore away from me, taking me for a steamer or a nondescript; but I gave chase, and getting over their scare, they hove to. I ran alongside and explained things. She proved to be the Norwegian barque "Franc," Captain Petersen; gave long. 25. W.

The captain knew my friend Modie in Boston. Also had read of us in the papers. Could not make us out. Had to rub his eyes a long time before he would believe that he was awake, and that we were really a legitimate Yankee craft. Wanted us to come on board, but we declined, and bidding him good-bye, shot under his bow, and in a moment were lying our course (which took him fifteen minutes to do), and were ready to "pass along another one." For the last week my chronometer watch has been useless to me, refusing to stay wound, something having given out inside of the works, leaving me without longitude or time of day—a very bad mishap.

Weather predictions by our barometer (my judgment) fair, set fair. Course E. by S. half S.

SEA SERPENT STORY.—
Wednesday, July 17th.
— Wind S. S. W.;
course E. by S. half S.;
sea smooth. These good weather spells kind of knock spots out of our ideas of making a quick passage. Just thirty-four days out. I never took much stock about sea serpents, but I have good reason to believe, after what I saw last evening, before dark, that there are denizens of the deep that have never been thoroughly explained or illustrated by our zoological societies. It was during a moment of intense calm, and I had been watching some whales sporting and spouting at a short distance behind me, when, on turning and looking in the opposite direction, I was startled to see what appeared to be a part of a huge

monster in the shape of a snake; it was about two hundred feet off. I saw twelve or fifteen feet of what appeared to be the tail of a huge black snake from five to fifteen inches in diameter, the end being stubby, or round, and white. It was in the air in a corrugated shape in motion, and in the act of descending. I also saw a dark shadowy form in the water corresponding with the tail; also the wake on the water as if more had just gone down, the whole being in motion after the manner of a snake; also heard the noise of the descending part, and saw the splash on the water.

Walter being just at that moment at the cuddy, where I keep the hatchet, getting some tea for supper, I told him to pass me the hatchet quick, which he did. He heard the splash and saw the form in the water. I wanted the hatchet, not because I thought I should have to use it, but because I thought it would be a good thing to have it handy, in case I should want to use it. Walter had a swim an hour before near the boat, and the thought of sea serpents being around kind of took away his relish for that kind of sport for the present.

During the night we heard from time to time the most horrid noises behind us that we have ever heard on the water—splashing and breathing in a loud wheezy manner, but that we took to be whales. This morning we saw and heard whales beating the water with their tails three miles off, throwing the water to a great distance in the air. We thought if they only saw fit to give the "Nautilus" one of those blows, that would settle our case here and save funeral expenses.

Thursday, July 18*th*.—Wind light, E. and S.E. At daylight saw three sails on horizon bound to westward. We spoke the middle one, the British brigantine "Nellie Crosby," of Yarmouth, N.S., Captain Bain, from England to Baltimore, Md., long. 24.30 W. Invited us on board to breakfast. Had a very sociable time; furnished us with a few luxuries we were in need of. No observation; rather chilly; we make but little easting. Last night Walter was taken with hæmorrhage, coughing up considerable quantities of blood; he said he felt better after it apparently; continued bleeding through the night at intervals. We made about thirty miles. Captain Bain said he had seen several sea serpents.

Friday, July 19th.—Light easterly winds, and we make considerable leeway; course doubtful. Passed between a brig and a brigantine about 8 a.m., bound west. Did not feel like speaking either of them, as we are in want of nothing but land. Fortune seems to have been against us from the send off, and we have given up all hopes of a quick passage. For twenty-six days the "Nautilus" did not rest a moment that she could sail; but our ignorance of certain localities, and having to heave to so often, everything being saturated with water, discouraged us. A quick passage is possible now, but not probable. Our health has been good beyond expectation, outside of Walter's hæmorrhage (I hardly understand *that*—he says he feels better every time after bleeding), neither of us being unable to perform our respective duties.

Although with a little reluctance for a moment sometimes, did we turn out of our "cubby hole" into the cold wet storm and dense darkness with fog, for eighteen consecutive days and nights that we passed without sun, moon, or stars to cheer us, to perform our task of four hours or more at the helm, to keep our faithful look-out before and behind, and to watch the compass with the utmost scrutiny without having been fairly asleep; and if sleep did come it was disturbed by dreams of a restless imagination that we were even then on duty, and had been for a week, and about to be relieved, instead of being off duty and about to go on.

No observation to-day, old Sol not turning out till too late, and then only showing the outlines of his welcome countenance. Course north by east. A few whales put in an appearance, and seemed to wonder what kind of a young visitor had dared to disturb the sanctity of their reservation. But seeing that we were decorous, no doubt they concluded to be so likewise, and permitted us to loiter around. While working out dead reckoning, a grampus, twenty-five feet long, gave us his unpleasant company, often coming within a few feet of us. Of course my little hatchet had to be brought into requisition. I made the remark to Walter that it was laying off our course under difficulties when we had to keep side-arms on top of the chart. He had numerous scars on his hide, reminding me of previous combats with foes no doubt, and I told him two were company enough for us and three a crowd, and that his room was better than his presence. At his departure I was relieved.

Wind W. Two ships ahead bound W. Changed our course to speak them. The first was the American ship "Annie H. Smith," of New York, Captain Roderick, from Hull, England, to New York, U.S.A. Lat. 48.06 N.; long. 24 W. Gave us his best wishes for success, and his last words that I could hear were, " Bully for you." The other was the British barque " J. B. Duffus," Captain Buckley, bound to Philadelphia, Penn. He said that he did not want to go to Havre with us. Wind N.E.; we stand to the southward. The bottom of the " Nautilus" is covered with barnacles, retarding our headway considerably. Passed two more ships in the night; tried to speak one of them, but he was afraid, and ran off. Walter's hæmorrhage is worse. Walter says he is not afraid to die, but he wants to get over first.

Saturday, July 20*th*.—Wind variable, all easterly and light. No observation to-day. Picked up six feet of the figure-head of some vessel; it was gilded and very handsome. No sails to-day. Rainbow in the morning, sailors take warning. "Scotch mist" and foggy, off and on. There is one thing certain; if we are not old sailors, we are old salts, our clothes being full of salt. The porpoises had great fun with us this evening, jumping out and falling on their backs and every way possible for them to. Run and course for the land somewhere. Walter's hæmorrhage continues. You can imagine my thoughts under the circumstances.

Sunday, July 21*st.*—Wind N., light and foggy. I managed by considerable perseverance to steal an observation to-day. Lat. 47.58 N.; long., dead reckoning, 20.30 W. Observed the Sabbath with one usual custom of our town, viz., baked beans and coffee for breakfast; we had no brown bread, the baker did not come round, and we could not get to Elm Square or Stickney's (at Beverly), so we made a virtue of necessity. Course E. by S. Five sails, and a few whales: "A rhyme, if you take it in time."

Plenty of tide-rips these twenty-four hours. We are working up to the course of the West Indiamen home to England for a change. Run about eighty miles. Spoke American barque "C. L. Carney," of New York, Captain Jackson, from New York to Dunkerque in France, with a cargo of kerosene oil. Went on board, took lunch and supper, and had a splendid time, the captain sparing no pains in our behalf, and will always be in my esteem a gentleman. Captain Jackson gave Walter a bottle of Friar's balsam, which stopped his bleeding after that, In the evening, a breeze springing up from the westward, I returned to the "Nautilus" and shot ahead of the barque, telling them I would report them in France, creating laughter; but the wind increasing I was compelled to soon follow in his wake, which I did for an hour, a lively conversation passing. But the large waves soon made me fall behind, to my regret.

> Oh, bury me not in the deep, deep sea;
> These words came low and mournfully
> At the close of the day, &c.

Monday, July 22nd.—Wind fresh from the south. Plenty of sails in sight. Going E. and W. Spoke British barque "Lizzie J. Leslie," of Liverpool, N.S., bound to Liverpool, England; lat. 47.22 N., long. 18.30 W., Captain Holbrook. Asked if I had my reckoning. Told him I had, and gave it to him. He said it was about right. Spoke German barque "Alster," of Hamburg, from New York to Hamburg, Captain Switzer. Spoke Norwegian barque "Floke," of Stavanager, Captain Englebretzen. Spoke American barque "Albina," of New York, Captain Goodfellow, bound to the port of Dunkerque, France. Spoke British ship "Annot Lyle," of Liverpool, England, from New York to Cork, Ireland, Captain Hinckley. At night it came on thick, and rain is no name for it. Oh, how it did blow! Hove to under sail at midnight. Chop sea running. Wind W., changed to N.N.W. Got under way again at 3 a.m. Run 215 miles. How is that for high speed?

Tuesday, July 23rd. — Wind W.N.W.; course E.S.E. Rain and mist with squalls. Making nine miles an hour. Hove to, and spoke Italian brig "Pape," bound to Queenstown, Ireland; Captain Nocomprehend, speakee too much Italian for us. Latitude 48.30 N.; longitude 17 W. The "Nautilus" is working now all she is good for. Saw a splendid meteor at night. When it burst it lit up all around like a sky-rocket. Passed a log twenty-five feet long and two feet in diameter, that would damage a ship if struck right—not to speak of our little half-inch boat. Also passed a trunk, skipjacks, and porpoises, dolphins, &c. Our "Nautilus" now reminds me of Longfellow's "Hiawatha," where "Every stride he strode a mile."

Wednesday, July 24th.—Wind N.W.; rain at intervals; heavy sea running. The "Nautilus" is doing her level best, under reefs, to get over this wet place, and it does seem that we are a long time. But time will tell, and blood too. Course E. by S. half S. Two sails passed us bound to the eastward. Very hard, but I got sight from old Sol to-day. Latitude by observation 48.18 N. We are off our course pretty bad, about fifteen miles from where I intended to be. Longitude, D.R., 14.30 W. There is more water between England and America than I ever dreamed of, especially when you come in a small boat like this. A little bad advice in regard to the current, which sets S.W. here, will explain everything. Tremendous long seas.

Thursday, July 25th.—Wind S.W., with fog and rain; wind shifted to N.W. Course by observation E.; latitude by observation 48.44 N.; longitude, D.R., 11.30 W. Passed two sails going to W.; fog lifted a spell. Had a wash up, &c. We have not done much fishing this trip, the extent of our catch being two nautili, one rudderfish, two barnacles off our boat's bottom, one bottle of wine, with two clubs tied to it, from a good captain, one Mother Carey's chicken (which flew into our sail and fell into my lap), and last night a skipjack jumped into Walter's lap while steering. Total, eight; so far, a curious fare for two fishermen, surely!

We have a rousing breeze from the N.W., making our miles to go less all the time. It does seem as though we were never to see the end of the ocean ahead. Spoke steamship "Daniel Steineman," of Antwerpen, Belgium, longitude 10.30 W. Said he would report us at Southampton, England. Hove to under sail, and remained most all night. Fearful high and bad seas. We are nearing Great Sole Bank, and are now on soundings. Bully for us. The "Nautilus" here threw her boom over the top of her mast three times, and we had to jibe here three or four times in order to get it back again.

Friday, July 26th.—Started at daylight, and ran on to the Great Sole Bank. Oh, what a place for a cockle-shell like this to be found in! I did all that anybody could do, but had to heave to with sail up, and finally was compelled to put out the drogue at 3 p.m., and remained all night. Saw two ships, close-reefed, bound to S.W. This is the worst we ever did see. Here we are in the middle of Rennel's Current, with a N.W. gale a-howling actually between life and death, and so near across too! More rain. The water was blown into smoke with the wind. Had to throw some oil this time for our lives, and no mistake! It is no wonder that the little "John T. Ford," of Baltimore, was lost in this vicinity by her ballast shifting. But few boats could live here under these circumstances, and the "Nautilus" has her hands full.

> "Yet rock'd in the cradle of the deep,
> In the 'Nautilus' I lay me down to sleep."

Saturday, July 27th.—Wind N.W. Rain and mist clouds. It moderates. We must get away from here if we have any regard for our lives. If we have not, this is a grand place to perish, and but One to know it! Ginger tea, hard bread, and the last of our salt beef do the work. Get under way at 9 a.m. After running twenty miles we spoke the French barque "St. Pierre," of Bordeaux (Captain Servet), from Monte Video, South America, for Falmouth, England. Saw two more sails bound E. and W. Captain Servet wanted to take us on board, boat and all, thinking that we were a French boat blown off from shore. Was pleased and surprised to find out that we were going to Paris. Latitude by observation 49.02 N.; longitude 8.20 W. Water quite sloppy now; forty-four days from home. Breezes up, and we lay our course for the Scilly Isles. Course E. by S.

Sunday, July 28th.—Wind comes around to S.E., which makes a bad, choppy sea, causing the "Nautilus" to pound awfully and quiver in every part of her, and a furious wind compels us to drift towards St. George's Channel. Hove to for an hour or so. At 3 p.m. got under way, and stood back into the English Channel. Could smell the new-mown hay, and knew by the great quantity of rock-weed, and the colour of the water, also the ground swell that was on, that we were in the vicinity of Old England. The mist lifting in the N.E. and S.W., we saw Bishop's Rock Lighthouse at 8 p.m., which makes us forty-five days from Thatcher's Island Lighthouse—the fastest time for any small sailing-boat. Hurrah for the "Nautilus"! We left Thatcher's Island, Cape Ann, at 9.30 p.m., June 12th, and made Bishop's Rock at 8 p.m., July 28th, just one hour and a half less than forty-five days.

Monday, July 29th.—Wind all round the compass. It moderates. Spoke Italian brig

"Giulietta" (Julietta), Captain Antonio Walinza, from Monte Video to Falmouth, England, latitude 47.19 N., longitude 6.25 W. Went alongside, and he gave us a drink of brandy and a bottle of wine. Wind to the eastward, and we make the Scillys again; go within a mile of some of the group. Spoke pilot boat "Gem," of the Scillys, a Channel groper; they wanted a job, but we declined. More fog and rain as usual. The Italian brig took a pilot and went to the N.W. of Scilly; we try to make the "Lizard" on the S.E. side. A very strong current is trying to carry us towards the islands, but with a fresh breeze from the north we object.

Tuesday, July 30th.—Make Runnelstone Head at daylight; wind N.E. "Thou art so near and yet so far." Spoke pilot-boat "Norman," of Falmouth. Wind died out, and we drifted out of sight of land. Air murky. Spoke two more pilot-boats. Make

The Land's End.

the land again near Penzance. Speak with some fishing-boats in regard to fish.

Wednesday, July 31*st.*—Made the Lizard Point at daylight, and stand out into the great race off the point. Wind E., and a spring tide; and this is the first time this voyage that I have been really surprised. Made up my mind that I knew but little about the English Channel, and did not want to know any more just now; but the "Nautilus" was good for it, and came out in two hours all right. Spoke schooner "Ierne," Capain Hooper, bound from Falmouth to Liverpool; he gave us a loaf of soft tack, and a can of corned beef; also some good advice in regard to Channel navigation. Many thanks.

We then sailed down the iron-bound coast of old Cornwall, the scene of hundreds of wrecks, not one of which ever got off; the place where in bygone days vessels were lured to destruction by means of false beacon-lights during storms; the cradle and hot-bed for smugglers and pirates; the home of Jack the Giant Killer; and a better abode for giants, seen as I now see it, could not be imagined. Bleak and desolate, with numerous caves—well, I will not undertake to describe the first land I made, or the Land's End; and I confess I had my mind occupied; and whether the old habits did not show up now occasionally I was in doubt, but I will put in and stand the consequences, be what they will; and seeing a small piece of sandy beach about forty feet long, thought it would be a good place for a swim, and till the wind would change; and so it was I went in with flying colours, and anchored within a few feet of an immense boulder to protect me from the wind, and such a din as the gulls and the wild birds set up I never heard.

It was Mullion Cove, coastguard and life-saving station. How fortunate we are safe! And now to a little toilet and some dinner, for it must be past noon, and I have not tasted a morsel to-day. After dinner a boat came alongside from the pilot cutter "Grand Turk," Captain George Cox, of Falmouth, and Jacob Harris heard for the first time that this was the "Nautilus," all the way from America.

Ideas rather confused! Can it be possible that America is across the sea? Why I used to think it was England. Ah, the situation is changed; yes, and such a change too. Walter took the jug and went ashore with Harris to get some water, and soon the new arrival was telegraphed to the ends of the earth. I then visited the "Grand Turk," and they did all in their power to make us comfortable. I declined to go on shore to-day, as my log and chart must be attended to.

Thursday, August 1st.—Wind E., blowing a gale. The Mounts Bay is full of storm-stayed shipping. It is very fortunate for us that we are here, or we should be blown clear off soundings, no doubt. Hauled the "Nautilus" on shore and scraped the barnacles from her bottom. They were over an inch long, and were all carried off by curiosity-seekers. A part of my log, 4000 words, was copied here, to be telegraphed to the *New York Herald* by special and district correspondents, by request of James Gordon Bennett, and also to London papers. Took dinner with coastguardsman Parland Griffiths. Took supper at the Old Inn, kept in town by Miss Mary Mundy, at the special invitation of Rev. E. G. Harvey, a "Friend in need and a friend indeed" to us.

Friday, August 2nd. — Wind E. Gale increasing. Bay full of shipping, including several steamships. Had chads for breakfast on board the "Grand Turk." I have a severe attack of indisposition. This part of England is renowned for its ancient remains, and I wish that I could personally inspect them. The church here, built in the fifteenth century, occupies the site of one built in the twelfth century. Got a trophy from the fount. The houses here are all built of stone and mortar whitewashed, about one storey and a half high. The "Nautilus" was photographed to-day. (This is the view given on our title-page.) Got some advice from Captain Edwards in regard to the Channel, and a guide-book.

Saturday, August 3rd. — Wind N.E. Some of the vessels left to-day to make a hitch farther up the coast, and not to be found here if the wind should veer to S.W., as it often does, for many mariners have rendered up their lives here under those circumstances; but as the barometer has not changed, and to-morrow being Sunday, I shall remain to attend a regular Church of England service by the Rev. E. G. Harvey. Rained at intervals during the day. I do not want to land again after I leave here till I get to Havre, France, and then I want a good spell on shore. Had a Cornish pastie for supper, and slept on board the "Nautilus."

It was my intention before starting to secure at least one porpoise and a shark, as trophies of the adventure, and for that purpose I procured a porpoise iron, or harpoon. I could have captured hundreds if so inclined; but as they were my constant *compagnons de voyage*, and served to occupy my atttention with their sportiveness, and knowing that if the whales had the desire to capture me they could, much easier than I could a porpoise, I decided that discretion was the better part of valour, and concluded that the golden rule of doing to others as we would that they should do to us would be the right principle after all; and my decision was, if the large fish would not molest me, I would not touch those in my power. An empty bottle, or even a cork floating on the water, often were welcomed by me as signs of civilization.

My greatest precaution, however, was to always have a sharp knife in my pocket, so that if the boat were capsized, and could not be righted again, I could cut a hole through her bottom, or the half-inch cedar, and so be able to reach my canned provisions. A can of Boston baked beans would be just as acceptable on one side as the other. But I never relished the idea of trying the experiment. Still, I always had an alternative for every disaster.

Sunday, August 4th.—Wind W., and light.

Got photographs of the "Nautilus," from a Helston photographer, who was showing a little Yankee enterprise. Took breakfast with friend Griffiths. Attended a very interesting service by the vicar, and then took dinner with him. A great many visit the "Nautilus." This is the only event that has happened here outside of shipwrecks for many years. Air murky and hazy. Put the boat in the water, and anchored off shore to be all ready to leave for Havre to-morrow morning if possible.

Monday, August 5th.—Wind E., and morning opened with rain. Friend Griffiths was our only audience on departure from Mullion Cove. A gloomy outlook at daylight. On our way to the Lizard Point wind veered to S.E. Passed the Stag Rocks, they breaking within forty feet of us. My previous experience had taught me this, and off the Lizard were signalled by the signal station operators. Wind S. Course E. by S. half S. Spoke pilot-boats—No. 1, of Plymouth, and No. 3, of Falmouth. The steamer "Flamingo," of Cork, saluted us. We pass many vessels during the day. Off Dodman's, or Deadman's, Point, spoke in the night a fishing-smack. Told us to have nothing to do with the land. Weather thick and rainy at intervals during the night. Wind E. Course S.E. and N.E. Beating up. Near morning passed the Eddystone Lighthouse.

Tuesday, August 6th.—Wind E. Foggy and drizzly. Wind S.E., wind S. Lay our course again. Water sloppy. Spoke British barque "Assel." Concluded to make the land and be sure of our position. Made Bolt Head, then laid our course for the Start Point; passed the point, and spoke pilot-boat No. 2, of Plymouth, the "Allow Me." They presented us with a

"Pilot's Guide Book of the Channel," and were very anxious to assist us. Such men deserved success. Portland then bore N.N.E. twenty miles. Told us to improve the wind, which was now S.W., with the appearance of bad weather. We sailed forty miles farther E. by S. half S., then changed our course to S. by E., and crossed the Channel to the iron-bound coast of France, the mariner's dread. Wind W.S.W.

Wednesday, August 7th.—Made the land between Cape La Hague and Cape Barfleur, sixty-five miles from Havre. Course now S.E. Spoke British steamer "Brunette," of London. They very kindly offered to tow us to Havre, but I thanked them and declined the favour, as I have often done before on like occasions. We are off Cherbourg, where, during our war of the rebellion, the "Kearsage" sunk the "Alabama" —only think, right on the same spot. We passed through the race of Cape Barfleur, which, luckily, was not bad considering everything. We passed another steamer, and some French pilot-boats. This morning it was rough and stormy, with considerable rain; afternoon very pleasant. Made Cape La Heve double lights, that can be seen eight leagues, at 9 p.m. Sailed till we were within two leagues of them, and hove to till daylight.

Thursday, August 8th.—Entered Havre, the fine seaport of Paris, this morning, with colours flying. We were met at the outer harbour by Mr. A. H. Thompson, of 385, Quai de Ille, to whom I had a letter of introduction from Mr. C. T. Woodbury. We took his boat, which was longer than ours, in tow, and under his pilotage entered the docks. Mr. Thompson attended to the Custom House first, and putting a keeper in the "Nautilus," and procuring a cab, proceeded to attend to

K

the inner as well as the outer man. We could not have had a better or more zealous friend, and we shall ever look upon him as only those in our condition can. It is holiday here for two days, and all the streets are gaily decorated with bunting of every description, and at night the public places are illuminated as only the French know how. The voyage of the "Nautilus" is over. We were three days from Land's End to Havre, making our time from Beverley to Havre forty-eight days.

We sleep to-night on a nice feather-bed, while the "Nautilus" calmly reposes in Mr. Cooper's dry dock. The smallest vessel ever in Havre from America before the "Nautilus" was a schooner of 213 tons. So Mr. Thompson informed me, showing me her photograph. The weight of the "Nautilus" is 600 lbs.

CHAPTER VI.

Remarks on the Log.

Such is the completed log of the "Nautilus," as copied out by William Andrews from his pencil entries in his pocket-book, day by day. It would have been easy to expand the narrative, as would have been done had the notes been put into the hand of a professional author to prepare for the press; but there is far more value, as well as real interest, in the plain, unvarnished tale, as told by William Andrews, when the matter was first in his memory, and the rough notes still legible. It only remains to add a few notes on the daring voyage, and the men who performed it.

On looking at the tiny craft, as we first saw it in the Brighton Aquarium, with planking only half an inch thick, our wonder was how it ever survived the perils of the ocean. It looks like a toy-boat, which the waves could not fail to overwhelm, and which any of the monsters of the deep could have knocked to pieces by an angry attack or a playful charge.

The endurance of the crew is even more wonderful than the frailness of their boat. In the little cabin there is not room for a grown man to turn over, and it afforded very partial rest or shelter. Day after day, and night after night, they wore their wet clothes unchanged; their sleep always brief and broken, and sometimes they had no rest for a week. They had the hot coffee only a few times in the forty-five days of the voyage, and could eat little. Chewing tobacco, after the manner of sailors, seemed their chief comfort, and may have lessened the nervous tension, as well as stayed their hunger. Their whole reserve force was exhausted in the task of getting across, and would not have sufficed for this, apart from their indomitable pluck and perseverance. These "Beverly boys" do credit to the physical constitution and adventurous spirit of the New England race.

These men, as has already been said, were not even sailors; they were artisans, or working men, with little nautical knowledge and experience. The eldest brother, William A. Andrews, was at this time thirty-five years of age, and his only experience as part of a ship's company had been one trip to the Grand Banks, taken more for his health and recreation than anything else, as he knew that his share of the receipts would be insufficient to meet the current expenses that would be incurred during his absence from home.

As Andrews belonged to a small town on the Bay of Massachusetts, his inexperience of the sea must be regarded as a neglect of early training, but his tastes were not in that line. He is a mechanic of some skill, and a man of an inquiring mind; a pianoforte-maker by trade, having worked for the well-known firm of Chickering and Sons, Boston, for about eight years, and other well-known manufacturers. He also is an old soldier, having served four years and three months during the late rebellion with distinction as colour-bearer, and being wounded three times. He has travelled a good deal through most of the States, and has been also in the British provinces, Mexico, Panama, and the West Indies.

The younger brother, Asa W. Andrews, was then twenty-three years of age, and had been to the fishing-ground several times, having had several narrow escapes from being lost. He is also a bit of a genius in his way, being able to turn his hands to many sorts of work—that which pays the best.

Neither of the men ever before took an observation of the sun for finding position at sea, and only claim to be average amateur boat sailors. Their first observation on board the "Nautilus," after her departure from Boston, is described in the log. Their quadrant was an old one, disused for many years, and sadly in want of repairs. Their chronometer was a watch, which broke down a few days from home, leaving them without time altogether. Their longitude could be found only by keeping dead reckoning, or speaking vessels when convenient, either being very defective oftentimes; their only knowledge of the course being from those of little or no experience. Their course took them into the "Cap Seas," or "Rolling Forties" of sailors, to the south and eastward of the Grand Banks, exposing them for weeks to the danger of being engulfed.

For eighteen days they were without sun, moon, or stars, and in the worst of weather. Their course was partly in the line of meeting between the Arctic current and Gulf Stream, where the water is always troubled, and ready for a commotion at the least wind in either direction. Their chart was an old second-hand one, without the information of those of a later date, and having many bugbears and obsolete rocks. They had a good compass, however, one of Baker's, of Boston; for small craft, they say there is not its equal, being of great power, and very steady under any circumstances.

With all their disadvantages, they made a straighter course across than seventy-five ships out of 100. They made the best time of any small sailing craft. The first third of the voyage took twenty-six days, the other two-thirds only nineteen days. With fair wind and weather, they say the voyage could be made in twenty-five days. From the meridian of Cape Race to Queenstown their sailing-time was only twenty-one days.

They counted fourteen separate storms, the first lasting four days, and the second five days. They drifted over 200 miles on their course backwards with a fair wind, and could not sail on account of the enormous combing waves in the second storm.

Many old sea-captains even now doubt that she came over by fair means, she being so slightly built, notwithstanding they spoke thirty-seven vessels on the passage, many of them in bad weather, all of which reported them. A list of the vessels spoken with is given in the Appendix. If this book falls into the way of any of the crews of these ships, they will remember with interest the little craft which caused so much surprise when met with on the ocean.

By a singular coincidence, the elder brother always said they would be forty-five days crossing the ocean.

The hardest task, they say, was the bidding adieu to family relations and friends before the immense throng of spectators assembled to see the start.

With the exception of the mysterious and unexplained apparition of one marine monster, which suggested recollections of "Sea Serpent" stories, there was nothing of an unusual kind met with during the voyage. There were the usual flying visitors in sea-birds of various species. Medusæ, and other marine animals, are familiar to all sailors, and especially the "Portuguese man-of-war," often loosely confounded with the nautilus of warm latitudes. Multitudes of these drifted along, with their tiny pink-vein, sail-like membranes open to the wind. Andrews maintains, however, that he saw the true nautilus also, and we give his own account, of which scientific readers may form their own judgment :—

" I have seen over a dozen different shapes of nautili. I saw at one time, while coming from San Francisco to New York (a passenger on board of the Pacific mail steamer 'Alaska') over a million of nautili, in fact for miles the steamer actually ploughed her way through them. I don't know what naturalists call *the* nautilus, but the nautilus that my boat is named after was often my companion while in the Gulf Stream. While in Paris, I saw several different kinds of shells from Australia with the word 'Nautilus' on them (and the word was clipped from my hand-bills to put upon them). I believe that even nautili of species belonging to southern latitudes may be brought to the North Atlantic. The equatorial current takes them along till they reach the coast of South America; they are then drawn into the Caribbean Sea, then into the Gulf of Mexico, then out into the Atlantic, in a north-easterly direction, till the banks of Newfoundland are met.

"A nautilus has little power of locomotion or propulsion. The old story of mariners that they have sails and oars, and can work to windward, is sheer fable. They are chiefly bladders, so to speak, full of air, but with long tentacles, perhaps a dozen, three feet, more or less, hanging down in the water, their means of subsistence. Probably the current of water is strong, the wind light, and the friction of the water on the tentacles is sufficient to force them to windwards.

"I have watched them while in my boat on several occasions when we were at the drogue and helpless. I saw them apparently sailing along splendidly, and as I would see a huge wave come combing along I would watch the effect on them. Many a time I have seen them thrown end over end for many feet, and after the wave had passed they would be on their side or capsized. But as the tentacles gradually sank down again they would come up right once more and gaily continue on to their destiny. I don't think they can exist in a low temperature; but if it is the will of the elements that they drift to a cold current of water, they must perish. Portuguese man-of-war is the name given often to nautili by sailors."

Whales occasionally caused anxiety, and not without good reason, their curiosity bringing them into closer proximity to the frail boat than was pleasant or safe. The droll pranks of playful porpoises afforded less perilous excitement. They are the very monkeys of the ocean, in constant and apparently aimless activity of motion. Sometimes they appeared as if charging right on to the boat, then darting off, bounding across the bows, and reappearing in the same tumultuous hurry at the stern.

No attempt was made at any scientific observations, either as to meteorology or natural history, the voyagers having no education in such matters; but the plain record of what was seen and experienced has many points of interest.

On one practical matter some useful experiments were made. Several times, when anchored by the drogue, and when the waves seemed perilous and threatening, the power of oil to calm the surface and to prevent breakers was satisfactorily tested. Having one gallon of cod-liver oil, about a quart being allowed to drip to leeward, the effect was to produce a smooth surface, beneath which the swelling waves passed, seldom breaking, even during a gale, at the place over which the oil had spread itself. Had a larger quantity been available, the effect would, no doubt, have been more marked.

The rig of the boat is the most primitive possible. She weighs less with everything in her than the ballast of the smallest boat that ever crossed before them, and is the only boat that ever crossed with only provisions and crew. The weight in all was about 600 lbs.

French papers compared the voyage as more like one of Jules Verne's than a reality. The voyagers were presented with an American flag on their arrival in Paris.

The "Nautilus" has no air or water-tight compartments, cork linings, caulking, self-righting, or life-saving apparatus of any kind.

At the race of the Oxford and Cambridge Universities boats' crews on the Thames, London, in April, 1879, the Andrews Brothers had the honour of flying the only American flag on the river, the hon. secretary of the Thames Sailing Club, Mr. Gus. Wright, kindly tendering them the services of his fine yacht, the "Oona," for the day. After the race the day was spent in a sail up and down the river.

At the close of the Paris Exposition, where it attracted much notice, the "Nautilus" was booked to the Royal Aquarium, Westminster, London, where it remained on exhibition a few days. It was then taken to Brighton. Here it remained till the autumn of 1879, when it was conveyed to Liverpool. The younger Andrews had already returned home, and the Captain, after some trouble, which he says has turned out for his good, and much anxiety as to getting his boat back to America, was kindly allowed to have it slung on board one of the Cunard liners, in which he worked his passage across. We hope he may long live to enjoy the fame and more substantial fruits of his enterprise.

In conclusion, one of the most interesting documents is the subjoined inventory of the outfit of the " Nautilus," beginning with—

PROVISIONS AND STORES.

60 galls. water, in 6 kegs ; 100 lbs. biscuits, in air-tight tins ; 30 cans Boston baked beans ; 10 cans tomatoes and peaches ; 10 cans green corn ; 10 cans green peas ; 7 cans St. Louis corned beef ; 1 can condensed milk ; 1 can grapes, preserved ; 1 can dried apples, preserved ; 1 can crab apples, preserved ; 1 can condensed beef ; 1 lb. tea ; 10 lb. coffee ; 2 lb. salt ; $\frac{1}{4}$ lb. pepper ; 1 lb. salts ; 10 lb. figs ; 2 lb. oatmeal ; 2 lb. Indian meal ; 2 bottles horse radish ; 1 bottle Renne's magic oil ; 2 bottles French mustard ; 1 doz. lemons ; 1 pepper-caster ; 1 fog-horn ; 1 mustard-spoon ; 1 loaf bread ; 1 loaf cake ; 1 ham ; 1 gross matches ; 4 knives ; 2 forks ; 2 spoons ; 1 coffee-pot ; 2 dippers ; 2

plates (tin); 6 galls. kerosene oil; 1 gall. alcohol; 1 gall. cod-liver oil, to lay the seas; 3 lanterns (white); 2 wooden buckets; 1 jug molasses; 1 jug vinegar; 1 jug for water; 4 boxes sardines; 1 box Ayer's cathartic pills; 20 lb. tobacco; 1 can-opener; 2 bottles Irish whiskey; 15 bottles laager beer; 5 clay pipes; 1 hammer; 1 hatchet; 1 saw; 4 bits; screws, nails, tacks.; screw-driver; boatswain's whistle; 1 life-belt, and other miscellaneous articles too numerous to mention; 2 suits of oil-clothes; 2 pr. rubber boots; 1 pr. mittens; 2 pr. wristers; 4 towels; 4 handkerchiefs; 1 bed-tick; 1 blanket; 1 pillow; 1 cushion; 1 mirror; 2 combs; 1 brush; 2 tooth-brushes; 1 wooden pump for water-kegs.

All our under-clothes, and two good suits of clothes, we threw away in England, being wet and mouldy.

Captain Edwards, of Mullyon, kindly

loaned me a Channel guide after my arrival there. Captain of Pilot Boat No. 2, of Plymouth, the " Allow Me," also presented me with a Pilot's guide of English side of the Channel.

NAUTICAL INSTRUMENTS.

1 chart, North Atlantic; 1 quadrant for taking lat. and long.; 1 chronometer watch, regulated to Greenwich time; 1 Baker's oil-compass, very nice; 1 ordinary air-compass; 1 boat-compass, or tell-tale; 2 compass-needles, my own manufacture; 1 parallel rule; 2 pr. dividers.

BOOKS AND WRITING MATERIALS.

1 Holy Bible; 1 Nautical Almanack, for getting sun's declination; 1 Bowditch's Navigation Book; 2 Pocket note-books; 1 box of stationery; 6 lead pencils.

MISCELLANEOUS.

2 pieces of leather, 1 piece of canvas, and 1 roll of marlin, for chaffing purposes; 1 15 lb. anchor; 1 canvas drogue, for heaving-to; 50 fathoms cable; 2 oars and rowlocks; 2 blocks; 1 American flag; 1 English Union Jack; 1 French flag; 1 sailor's clothes-bag; 1 sailor's hammock (we used it to keep our clothes off from the side of the boat); 1 fair leader; 2 spruce poles, for repairing; 1 storm sail (try-sail); 1 cod-fish line; 1 small-fish line; 1 log-book, or memorandum; 1 pr. cutting pliers; 1 razor; 1 roll copper wire; 1 small screw-driver; 2 files; 1 hammer; 1 hatchet; 1 saw; 1 plane; 1 coffee-pot; 1 stewpan; 1 funnel; 2 plates (tin); 2 dippers (tin); 1 jar for matches (airtight); 1 2-foot rule; 2 bottles whiskey (Irish), for sickness only; 1 wooden pipe, Walter made on the passage; 1 roll of spare rope;

1 watch-key; 1 kerosene oil-stove (a nuisance); 1 alcohol lamp (a good thing); 1 sponge; 1 six-shot revolver; 2 dozen screw-eyes; 2 dols. in greenbacks, ½ dol. in silver.

We had also six letters to mail to different persons in England on arrival.

Among the documents authenticating the voyage are the Custom House certificates on departure from Boston and arrival at Havre.

Custom House, Boston, Mass.
Collector's Office,
June 6th, 1878.

To whom it may concern.

The bearer, William A. Andrews, informs me that he intends starting for Havre, France, on Friday next, in the Dory "Nautilus," dimensions 19 feet long, 6 feet 7 inches wide, 2 feet 3 inches deep, with Asa W. Andrews for assistant. This is given to show that at this date Mr. Andrews is in my office, and is known to me.

ALANSON W. BEARD,
Collector of the Port of Boston.

Havre, France,
August 9th, 1878.

Dr. The American Boat "Nautilus,"
To H. Franque, Ship-broker.

Board of Health	30c.
Custom House duties and clearance, &c.	3f.25c.
	3f.55c.

République Française.

Douanes, Port du Havre. Passe-port des Navires Étrangers, No. 1754, du Régistre de Recette.

Au nom du Président de la République.

L'Administration des Douanes Françaises donne, par les présentes, au Sr. Wm. A. Andrews, du yacht Américain "Nautilus," de 1 tonnage 50, Passe-port et permission de sortie du port ci-dessus désigné, après avoir subi la visite ordinaire, tant du navire que de sa cargaison, pour aller à Paris. Pour lequel Passe-port, tenant lieu d'un certificat, il a payé, aux termes de la loi du 27 Vendémiaire, An 2, Art. 37, un franc, outre le droit du timbre.

Delivré au Bureau des Douanes le 8 Août, 1878, au Ministère des Finances.

V. LEESHAM.

The "Nautilus" has been on exhibition at Boston since its return to America, and Captain W. Andrews has had several offers to take it to other places. He has preferred meanwhile to work quietly at his trade, and to enjoy the comforts of home. But in his latest letter he says, "You may hear of my attempting something again, inside of ten years, if I live."

LONDON:
GILBERT AND RIVINGTON, PRINTERS,
ST. JOHN'S SQUARE.

A CATALOGUE OF
NEW & POPULAR WORKS,

AND OF BOOKS

FOR CHILDREN,

SUITABLE FOR PRESENTS AND SCHOOL PRIZES.

NEW YORK:

E. P. DUTTON & CO.,

GRIFFITH & FARRAN, ST. PAUL'S CHURCHYARD, LONDON.

5M. 6.80. *Cancelling all previous Editions of this Catalogue.*

CONTENTS.

	PAGE
New Books and New Editions, 1879—80	3
New Fiction	7
Poetry	7
Stanesby's Illuminated Gift Books	8
Birthday Books...	8
Manuals on Confirmation, &c.	9
New Books and New Editions for Children...	9
One Dollar Seventy-five Cent Books	11
One Dollar Fifty Cent Books	11
One Dollar Twenty-five Cent Books	14
One Dollar Books	18
Seventy-five Cent Books	22
Fifty Cent Books	23
Forty Cent Books	24
The Favourite Library	25
Durable Nursery Books	26
Tiny Natural History Series...	27
Taking Tales	27
Works for Distribution	28
Educational Works	29

NEW BOOKS AND NEW EDITIONS.

SIX LIFE STUDIES OF FAMOUS WOMEN.
By M. BETHAM-EDWARDS, author of "Kitty," "Dr. Jacob," "A Year in Western France, etc. With six Portraits engraved on Steel. Cloth, price $2.25.

THE FOLK-LORE OF SHAKESPEARE.
By the Rev. T. F. THISTLETON DYER, M.A., author of "British Popular Customs" and "English Folk-Lore." The following is an outline of the subjects, and the manner in which they are grouped :—
    Introduction. Chapter I.—Life of Man. (*a*) Birth, Baptism, Childhood. (*b*) Marriage. (*y*) Death, Burial. II.—The Human Body. III.—Charms and Spells, Divinations and Auguries. IV.—Day and Seasons. V.—Weather-Lore, Sun, Moon, Rainbow, Stars, Comets, Thunder, Winds, Squalls, Clouds, &c. VI.—Birds. VII.—Animals. VIII.—Insects. Reptiles, Fish. IX.—Plants. X.—Witches. XI.—Fairies. XII.—Ghosts and Spirits. XIII.—Dreams. XIV.—Sundry Superstitions. XV.—Sports and Pastimes. XVI.—Fools.

THE FOLK-LORE OF OLD JAPAN: a
Budget of Notes about Nipon. By C. PFOUNDES.
    Mr. Pfoundes has lived for over twelve years with the Japanese people, has mastered the colloquial, and has lived the native life amongst the intelligent better class in that country. Adopting that which is best in the classifications of the leading folk-lore authorities, Mr. Pfoundes does not profess to make an exhaustive collection, but simply to give under each heading the most characteristic illustrations derived from the native literature and his own observations, in the hope that others may be induced to follow this most fruitful branch of study.

WOTHORPE BY STAMFORD. A Tale of
Bygone Days. By C. HOLDICH. With five Engravings. Crown 8vo, cloth, price $1.25.

THE BICYCLE ROAD BOOK: compiled
for the use of Bicyclists and Pedestrians, being a Complete Guide to the Roads of England, Scotland, and Wales, with a list of the best Hotels and notable places on each journey, population, &c. By CHARLES SPENCER, author of "The Modern Gymnast," "The Modern Bicycle," &c. Cloth, limp, 75c.

THE ART OF WASHING; Clothes, Personal, and House. By Mrs. A. A. STRANGE BUTSON, Author of "On the Leads." 50c.

AMBULANCE LECTURES: or, what to do
in cases of Accidents or Sudden Illness. By LIONEL A. WEATHERLY, M.D., Lecturer to the Ambulance Department, Order of St. John of Jerusalem in England. With numerous Illustrations. Dedicated (by permission) to the Ambulance Department of the Order of St. John of Jerusalem in England. Third Thousand, sewed, price 40c.

NEW AND POPULAR WORKS

DEACONESSES IN THE CHURCH OF England. A Short Essay on the order as in the Primitive Church, and on their position and work. Revised by the Very Reverend the Dean of Chester.

GLIMPSES OF THE GLOBE. A First Geographical Reader for Children. By J. R. BLAKISTON, Author of "The Teacher," &c. 40c.

> By the use of this little volume of dialogues as a class reading book, it is believed that children, even under inexperienced teachers, will unconciously and pleasantly gain some knowledge of the earth's surface and movement.

PLAIN HINTS FOR THOSE WHO HAVE to Examine Needlework, whether for Government Grants, Prize Associations, or Local Managers, to which is added Skeleton Demonstration Lessons to be used with the Demonstration Frames, and a glossary of terms used in the Needlework required from the scholars in public elementary schools. By the EXAMINER OF NEEDLEWORK TO THE SCHOOL BOARD FOR LONDON. Price 75c.

EIGHT MONTHS IN AN OX-WAGGON: Reminiscences of Boer Life. By EDWARD F. SANDEMAN. Demy 8vo., cloth, with a Map, $3·50.

TRAVEL, WAR, AND SHIPWRECK. By COLONEL W. PARKER GILLMORE ("UBIQUE,") Author of "The Great Thirst Land," &c. Demy 8vo. $2·50.

POLITICIANS OF TO-DAY. A Series of Personal Sketches. By T. WEMYSS REID, Author of "Charlotte Brontë; a Monograph." Cabinet Portraits, &c. Two Vols., Crown 8vo., cloth, $3·50.

RECORDS OF YORK CASTLE, FORTress, Court House, and Prison. By A. W. TWYFORD (the present Governor) and Major ARTHUR GRIFFITHS, author of "The Memorials of Millbank." Crown 8vo. With Engravings and Photographs. $1·75.

THE BIRTHDAY BOOK OF QUOTATIONS and Autograph Album. Extracts in English, French, and German, chiefly from standard authors. With Calendar, Ornamental Borders for Photographs, Album for Translations, and Chosen Mottoes. Extra cloth and gilt, price $3·00.

CREWEL WORK. Fifteen designs in Bold and Conventional Character, capable of being quickly and easily worked. With complete instructions. By ZETA, Author of "Ladies Work and How to Sell it," and including Patterns for Counterpanes, Bed Hangings, Curtains, Furniture Covers, Chimney-piece Borders, Piano Backs, Table Cloths, Table Covers, &c., &c. Demy. In an Envelope, price $1·00.

PICTURES OF THE PAST: Memories of
Men I Have Met, and Sights I Have Seen. By FRANCIS H.
GRUNDY, C.E. One vol., Crown 8vo., cloth., price $3·50.

Contains personal recollections of Patrick Branwell Brontë, Leigh Hunt and his family, George Henry Lewes, George Parker Bidder, George Stephenson, and many other celebrities, and gives besides descriptions of very varied experiences in Australia.

STORIES from EARLY ENGLISH LITERATURE, with some Account of the Origin of Fairy Tales, Legends and Traditionary Lore. Adapted to the use of Young Students. By Miss S. J. VENABLES DODDS. Cr. 8vo., price $1·75.

THE LIFE MILITANT: Plain Sermons for Cottage Homes. By ELLELL. Crown 8vo., price $1·75.

HOFER: A Drama. By CATHERINE SWANWICK. Demy 8vo., cloth, gilt edges, price $1·25.

RICHARD CŒUR DE LION. A Legendary Drama. By CATHERINE SWANWICK, Author of "Hofer," &c. Cloth, gilt edges, price $1·25.

HISTORICAL SKETCHES OF THE REFORMATION. By the Rev. FREDERICK GEO. LEE, D.C.L., Vicar of All Saints', Lambeth, &c., &c., &c. One Volume, post octavo, $4·00.

THE COMMERCIAL PRODUCTS OF THE SEA; or, Marine Contributions to Industry and Art. By P. L. SIMMONDS, Author of "The Commercial Products of the Vegetable Kingdom." One vol., with numerous Illustrations, $5·00.

A GLOSSARY OF BIOLOGICAL, ANATOMICAL, AND PHYSIOLOGICAL TERMS, for Teachers and Students in Schools and Classes connected with the Science and Art Department, and other Examining bodies. By THOMAS DUNMAN, Physiology Lecturer at the Birkbeck Institution and the Working Men's College. Crown 8vo., cloth $1·00.

THE CRIMEAN CAMPAIGN WITH THE CONNAUGHT RANGERS, 1854-55-56. By Lieut.-Colonel NATHANIEL STEEVENS, late 88th (Connaught Rangers). One volume, Demy 8vo., with Map, Scarlet Cloth, $5·00.

"A welcome addition to the military history of England."—
United Service Gazette.

MEMORABLE BATTLES IN ENGLISH HISTORY: The Military Lives of the Commanders. By W. H. DAVENPORT ADAMS. With Frontispiece and Plans of Battles. Two vols., Crown 8vo., Cloth. Price $5·00.

OCEAN AND HER RULERS: A Narrative
of the Nations which have from the Earliest Ages held Dominion over the Sea, comprising a Brief History of Navigation from the Remotest Periods up to the Present Time. By ALFRED ELWES. With 16 Illustrations by W. W. MAY. Cr. 8vo. Price $3·50.

MASTERPIECES OF ANTIQUE ART.
From the celebrated collections in the Vatican, the Louvre, and the British Museum. By STEPHEN THOMPSON, Author of "Old English Homes," &c. Twenty-five Examples in Permanent Photography. Super-Royal Quarto. Elegantly bound, price $10·00.

WORKS BY JOHN TIMBS, F.S.A.

Notabilia, or CURIOUS AND AMUSING FACTS ABOUT MANY THINGS. Explained and Illustrated by JOHN TIMBS, F.S.A. Post 8vo, $1·75.
"There is a world of wisdom in this book."—*Art Journal.*

Ancestral Stories and Traditions of Great Families. Illustrative of English History. With Frontispiece. Post 8vo, price $2·00.
"An interesting and well written book."—*Literary Churchman.*

Strange Stories of the Animal World. A Book of Curious Contributions to Natural History. Illustrations by ZWECKER. Second Edition. Post 8vo, gilt edges, price $1·75.
"Will be studied with profit and pleasure."—*Athenæum.*

The Day Dreams of a Sleepless Man: being a series of Papers contributed to the *Standard*, by FRANK IVES SCUDAMORE, Esq., C.B. Post 8vo, price $1·25.

Mission from Cape Coast Castle to Ashantee. WITH A DESCRIPTIVE ACCOUNT OF THAT KINGDOM. By the late T. EDWARD BOWDICH, ESQ. With preface by his daughter, Mrs. HALE. With map of the route to Coomassie. $1·50.

Joan of Arc AND THE TIMES OF CHARLES THE SEVENTH. By Mrs. BRAY, Author of "Life of Stothard," etc. Post 8vo, price $2·00.
"Readers will rise from its perusal, not only with increased information, but with sympathies awakened and elevated."—*Times.*

The Good St. Louis and His Times. By Mrs. BRAY. With Portrait. Post 8vo, price $2·00.
"A valuable and interesting record of Louis' reign."—*Spectator.*

Sagas from the Far East, or KALMOUK AND MONGOLIAN TALES. With Historical Preface and Explanatory Notes by the Author of "Patrañas," etc. Post 8vo, price $2·50.

The Vicar of Wakefield; a Tale by OLIVER GOLDSMITH. With eight Illustrations by JOHN ABSOLON. Beautifully printed by Whittingham. $1·25 cloth.

STORIES FOR DAUGHTERS AT HOME.

Cloth, price $1·25.

Kind Hearts. By Mrs. J. F. B. FIRTH, Author of "Sylvia's New Home," &c. With Frontispiece.

Very Genteel. By the Author of "Mrs. Jerningham's Journal."

Stephen the Schoolmaster. A STORY WITHOUT PLOT. By Mrs. GELLIE (M. E. B.)

My Sister's Keeper; A STORY FOR GIRLS. In one vol. By LAURA M. LANE, Author of "Gentleman Verschoyle," &c. With a Preface by Mrs. TOWNSEND, President of the Girls' Friendly Society.

My Mother's Diamonds. By MARIA J. GREER. With a Frontispiece by A. LUDOVICI.

"Bonnie Lesley." By Mrs. HERBERT MARTIN, Author of "Cast Adrift, &c." With Frontispiece by Miss C. PATERSON.

Left Alone; or, THE FORTUNES OF PHILLIS MAITLAND. By FRANCIS CARR, Author of "Not Lancelot, nor another," &c.

St. Nicolas Eve and other Tales. By MARY C. ROWSELL. Crown 8vo. Price $2·25.

Fifty Years in Sandbourne. A SKETCH. By CECILIA LUSHINGTON. Fcap. 8vo., cloth, 50c.

POETRY.

Ambition's Dream. A POEM IN TWO FYTTES. New Edition. Fcap. 8vo., cloth, $1·00.

Poems. By E. L. FLOYER. Fcap. 8vo, price $1·25.

The Seasons; a Poem by the Rev. O. RAYMOND, LL.B. Fcap. 8vo, with Four Illustrations. Price $1·25.

STANESBY'S ILLUMINATED GIFT BOOKS.

Every page richly printed in Gold and Colours.

The **Bridal Souvenir.** New Edition, with a Portrait of the Princess Royal. Elegantly bound in white morocco, price $5·00.
"A splendid specimen of decorative art, and well suited for a bridal gift."

The **Birth-Day Souvenir.** A Book of Thoughts on Life and Immortality. Price $3·50 cloth; $4·50 morocco antique.

Light for the Path of Life; from the Holy Scriptures. Small 4to, price $4·00 cloth.

The **Wisdom of Solomon;** from the Book of Proverbs. Small 4to, price $4·50, cloth elegant.

The **Floral Gift.** Price $4·50 cloth.

Shakespeare's Household Words. With a Photograph from the Monument at Stratford-on-Avon. New and Cheaper Edition, Price $1·50, cloth elegant.

Aphorisms of the Wise and Good. With a Photographic Portrait of Milton. Price $1·50, cloth elegant.

THREE BIRTHDAY BOOKS.

I. The **Book of Remembrance** for every Day in the Year. With blank space for recording Birthdays, Weddings, &c., &c. Beautifully printed in red and black. Imp. 32mo., prices from $1·00 upwards.

II. The **Churchman's Daily Remembrancer.** With Poetical Selections for the Christian Year, with Calendar and Table of Lessons of the English Church, for the use of both Clergy and Laity. Cloth elegant, price $1·00.

III. The **Anniversary Text Book of Scripture Verse and Sacred Song** for Every Day in the Year. Cloth, 50c.

Emblems of Christian Life. Illustrated by W. HARRY ROGERS, in One Hundred Original Designs, from the Writings of the Fathers, Old English Poets, &c. Printed by Whittingham, with Borders and Initials in Red. Square 8vo. price $2·50. cloth elegant, gilt edges.

Caxton's Fifteen O's and other Prayers. Printed by command of the Princess Elizabeth, Queen of England and France, and also of the Princess Margaret, mother of our Sovereign Lord the King. By WM. CAXTON. Reproduced in Photo-Lithography by S. Ayling. Quarto, bound in parchment. New and cheaper edition, price $1·75.

Bishop Ken's Approach to the Holy Altar. With an Address to Young Communicants. Superior cloth, red edges, 50c.

Confirmation; or Called, and Chosen, and Faithful. By the Author of "The Gospel in the Church's Seasons" series. With a Preface by The Very Reverend the DEAN OF CHESTER. Fcap. 8vo., Cloth, 50c.

NEW BOOKS FOR CHILDREN

A DARING VOYAGE ACROSS THE ATLANTIC. By two Americans, the Brothers ANDREWS, in a Small Boat, less than 20 feet long, 6 broad, and 3 deep. The log of the Voyage by Captain WILLIAM A. ANDREWS. With Introduction and Notes by Dr. MACAULAY, Editor of the "Boys' Own Paper."

SEVEN STORIES about Old Folks and Young Ones. By A. R. HOPE, Author of "Buttons," &c. Crown 8vo., cloth, $1·75.

THE FAVOURITE PICTURE BOOK, and Nursery Companion. Compiled anew by UNCLE CHARLIE. With four hundred and fifty Illustrations by ABSOLON, ANELAY, BENNETT, BROWNE (PHIZ), SIR JOHN GILBERT, T. LANDSEER, LEECH, PROUT, HARRISON WEIR, and others. Medium 4to, cloth elegant, price $2·00, or coloured Illustrations, gilt edges, $4·00.

Also published in the following four parts, price 25c. each, or coloured Illustrations, 50c. :—

| THE PICTURESQUE PRIMER. | EASY READING FOR LITTLE READERS. |
| FRAGMENTS OF KNOWLEDGE FOR LITTLE FOLK. | THE NURSERY COMPANION. |

Each in an attractive Paper Cover.

The Bird and Insects Post Office. By ROBERT BLOOMFIELD. Illustrated with Thirty-five Illustrations. Crown 4to., cloth, $1.75., fancy board covers, $1.25.

Little Margaret's Ride to the Isle of Wight; or, THE WONDERFUL ROCKING HORSE. By Mrs. FREDERICK BROWN. With Eight Illustrations in chromo-lithography, by HELEN S. TATHAM. Crown 4to., cloth, $1·75., fancy boards, $1·25.

NEW AND POPULAR WORKS

Three Dollars Fifty Cents each, cloth elegant.

GOLDEN THREADS FROM AN ANCIENT LOOM; *Das Nibelungenlied* adapted to the use of Young Readers. By LYDIA HANDS. Dedicated by permission to THOMAS CARLYLE. With Fourteen Wood Engravings by J. SCHNORR, of Carolsfeld. Royal 4to.

CHILD LIFE IN JAPAN, and Japanese Child Stories. By M. CHAPLIN AYRTON. With Seven full-page Illustrations, drawn and engraved by Japanese artists, and many smaller ones. Quarto.

"People who give it away are likely to be tempted to buy a new copy to keep."—*Saturday Review.*

Two Dollars each, cloth elegant.

THE YOUNG BUGLERS: A Tale of the Peninsular War. By G. A. HENTY, Author of "Out on the Pampas," &c. With Eight full-page pictures by J. PROCTOR, and numerous plans of Battles. Large Crown 8vo.

THE MEN OF THE BACKWOODS: or, Stories and Sketches of the Indians and the Indian Fighters. By ASCOTT R. HOPE, author of "Heroes of Young America," &c., &c. Thirty-three Illustrations by C. O. MURRAY. Crown 8vo.

One Dollar Seventy-five Cents each, cloth elegant, with Illustrations.

*Kingston's (W. H. G.) Will Weatherhelm**: or, The Yarn of an Old Sailor about his Early Life and Adventures.
* ,, The Missing Ship, or Notes from the Log of the "Ouzel Galley."
* ,, The Three Admirals, and the Adventures of their Young Followers.
* ,, The Three Lieutenants; or, Naval Life in the Nineteenth Century.
* ,, The Three Commanders; or, Active Service Afloat in Modern Times.
* ,, The Three Midshipmen. New Edition, with 24 Illustrations by G. Thomas, Portch, etc.
* ,, Hurricane Hurry, or The Adventures of a Naval Officer during the American War of Independence.
* ,, True Blue; or, The Life and Adventures of a British Seaman of the Old School.

Ice Maiden and other Stories. By Hans Christian Andersen. 39 Illustrations by Zwecker. 4to., *Gilt edges.*

*Journey to the Centre of the Earth. Authorized Translation. From the French of Jules Verne. With 53 Illustrations.

Seven Stories about Old Folks and Young Ones. By A. R. Hope (Not illustrated.)

Little Maids. Rhymes with Illustrations by Mrs. W. Kemp. Quarto, gilt edges.

The Books marked * may be had with bevelled boards, gilt edges, price $2·25.

One Dollar Fifty Cents each, cloth elegant; or One Dollar Seventy-five Cents gilt edges. Illustrated by eminent Artists.

Chums: A Story for the Youngsters, of Schoolboy Life and Adventure. By Harleigh Severne.

Early Start in Life (The). By Emilia Marryat Norris.

Gentleman Cadet (The): His Career and Adventures at the Royal Academy, Woolwich. By Lieut.-Colonel Drayson.

Gerald and Harry, or The Boys in the North. By Emilia Marryat Norris.

NEW AND POPULAR WORKS

One Dollar Fifty Cents each—continued.

Hair-Breadth Escapes, or THE ADVENTURES OF THREE BOYS IN SOUTH AFRICA. By the Rev. H. C. ADAMS.

Heroes of the Crusades. By BARBARA HUTTON.

Home Life in the Highlands. By LILIAS GRAEME.

Household Stories from the land of Hofer, or POPULAR MYTHS OF TIROL, INCLUDING THE ROSE GARDEN OF KING LARYN.

Kingston's (W. H. G.) John Deane of Nottingham, HIS ADVENTURES AND EXPLOITS.

    „   **Rival Crusoes (The).** (*Or bevelled boards, gilt edges, $1·75.*)

Out on the Pampas, or THE YOUNG SETTLERS. By G. A. HENTY.

Patrañas, or SPANISH STORIES, LEGENDARY AND TRADITIONAL. By the Author of "Household Stories."

Swift and Sure, or THE CAREER OF TWO BROTHERS. By A. ELWES.

Tales of the Saracens. By BARBARA HUTTON.

Tales of the White Cockade. By BARBARA HUTTON.

Wilton of Cuthbert's: A TALE OF UNDERGRADUATE LIFE THIRTY YEARS AGO. By the Rev. H. C. Adams.

Workman and Soldier. A TALE OF PARIS LIFE DURING THE SIEGE AND THE RULE OF THE COMMUNE. By JAMES F. COBB, (or bevelled boards, gilt edges, $1·75.)

Young Franc Tireurs (The), AND THEIR ADVENTURES DURING THE FRANCO-PRUSSIAN WAR. By G. A. HENTY, Special Correspondent of the *Standard*.

One Dollar Fifty Cents each, cloth, Illustrated, gilt edges.

Elwes' (A.) Luke Ashleigh, or SCHOOL LIFE IN HOLLAND.

    „   **Paul Blake,** or A BOY'S PERILS IN CORSICA AND MONTE CRISTO.

Neptune's Heroes, or THE SEA KINGS OF ENGLAND, FROM HAWKINS TO FRANKLIN. By W. H. DAVENPORT ADAMS.

Talks about Plants, or EARLY LESSONS IN BOTANY. By Mrs LANKESTER. With six Coloured Plates and numerous Wood Engravings.

A NEW UNIFORM SERIES OF $1·50 VOLS.
Square Crown 8vo., gilt edges.

The Day of Wonders: A MEDLEY OF SENSE AND NONSENSE. By M. SULLIVAN. 30 Illustrations by W. G. BROWNE.

Harty the Wanderer; or, CONDUCT IS FATE. A Tale by FAIRLEIGH OWEN. 28 Illustrations by JOHN PROCTOR.

A Wayside Posy. GATHERED FOR GIRLS. By F. LABLACHE. 15 Illustrations by A. H. COLLINS.

One Dollar Fifty Cents each, cloth elegant, Illustrated.

Extraordinary Nursery Rhymes; New, yet Old. Translated from the Original Jingle into Comic Verse by One who was once a Child. 60 Illustrations. Small 4to.

Little Gipsy (The). By ELIE SAUVAGE. Translated by ANNA BLACKWELL. Profusely illustrated by ERNEST FRÖLICH. Small 4to, ; (or, extra cloth, *gilt edges*, $1·75.)

Norstone; or, RIFTS IN THE CLOUDS. By M. E. HATTERSLEY.

Merry Songs for Little Voices. Words by Mrs. BRODERIP. Music by THOMAS MURBY. With 40 Illustrations. Fcap. 4to.

Stories from the Old and New Testaments. By the Rev. B. H. DRAPER. With 48 Engravings.

Trimmer's History of the Robins. Written for the Instruction of Children on their treatment of Animals. With 24 Illustrations by HARRISON WEIR. Small 4to, gilt edges.

One Dollar Fifty Cents each, cloth elegant, with Illustrations.

Alda Graham; and her Brother Philip. By E. MARRYAT NORRIS.

Book of Cats (The): a Chit-chat Chronicle of Feline Facts and Fancies. By CHARLES H. ROSS.

"Buttons." THE TRIALS AND TRAVELS OF A YOUNG GENTLEMAN. By ASCOTT R. HOPE.

Casimir, the Little Exile. By CAROLINE PEACHEY.

Cornertown Chronicles. NEW LEGENDS OF OLD LORE WRITTEN FOR THE YOUNG. By KATHLEEN KNOX.

Favourite Fables in Prose and Verse. With 24 beautiful Illustrations from Drawings by HARRISON WEIR. Small 4to.

Fiery Cross (The), OR THE VOW OF MONTROSE. By BARBARA HUTTON.

One Dollar Fifty Cents each—continued.

Mandarin's Daughter (The): A STORY OF THE GREAT TAEPING REBELLION. By SAMUEL MOSSMAN.

Modern British Plutarch (The), or LIVES OF MEN DISTINGUISHED IN THE RECENT HISTORY OF OUR COUNTRY FOR THEIR TALENTS, VIRTUES, AND ACHIEVEMENTS. By W. C. TAYLOR, LL.D.

Oak Staircase, (The) or THE STORIES OF LORD AND LADY DESMOND a Narrative of the Times of James II. By M. and C. LEE.

Royal Umbrella (The). By MAJOR A. F. P. HARCOURT, Author of "The Shakespeare Argosy," &c., &c. With 4 full page Illustrations by LINLEY SAMBOURNE. $1·50.

Silver Linings: or, LIGHT AND SHADE. By Mrs. REGINALD M. BRAY.

Tales and Legends of Saxony and Lusatia. By W. WESTALL.

Theodora: a Tale for Girls. By EMILIA MARRYAT NORRIS.

Zipporah, the Jewish Maiden. By M. E. BEWSHER.

One Dollar Twenty-five Cents plain; or coloured plates and gilt edges, One Dollar Fifty Cents Super Royal 16mo, cloth elegant, with Illustrations.

Aunt Jenny's American Pets. By CATHERINE C. HOPLEY.

Broderip (Mrs.) Crosspatch, the Cricket, and the Counterpane.
　　,, **My Grandmother's Budget** OF STORIES AND VERSES.
　　,, **Tales of the Toys.** TOLD BY THEMSELVES.
　　,, **Tiny Tadpole,** AND OTHER TALES.

Cousin Trix, AND HER WELCOME TALES. By GEORGIANA CRAIK.

Cosmorama: THE MANNERS AND CUSTOMS OF ALL NATIONS OF THE WORLD DESCRIBED. By J. ASPIN.

Distant Homes, or THE GRAHAM FAMILY IN NEW ZEALAND. By Mrs. I. E. AYLMER.

Early Days of English Princes. By Mrs. RUSSELL GRAY.

Echoes of an Old Bell. By the Hon. AUGUSTA BETHELL.

Facts to Correct Fancies, or SHORT NARRATIVES OF REMARKABLE WOMEN.

Fairy Land, or RECREATION FOR THE RISING GENERATION, in Prose and Verse. By THOMAS and JANE HOOD. Illustrated by T. HOOD, Jun.

Feathers and Fairies, or STORIES FROM THE REALMS OF FANCY. By the Hon. AUGUSTA BETHELL.

Garden (The), or FREDERICK'S MONTHLY INSTRUCTION FOR THE MANAGEMENT AND FORMATION OF A FLOWER GARDEN. With Illustrations by SOWERBY. ($1·75. *coloured.*)

One Dollar Twenty-five Cents each—continued.

Hacco the Dwarf, or THE TOWER ON THE MOUNTAIN, and other Tales. By LADY LUSHINGTON.

Happy Home (The), or THE CHILDREN AT THE RED HOUSE. By LADY LUSHINGTON.

Helen in Switzerland. By the Hon. AUGUSTA BETHELL.

Holidays among the Mountains, or SCENES AND STORIES OF WALES. By M. BETHAM EDWARDS.

Lightsome and the Little Golden Lady. Written and Illustrated by C. H. BENNETT. Twenty-four Engravings.

Nursery Times, or STORIES ABOUT THE LITTLE ONES. By an Old Nurse.

Play Room Stories, or HOW TO MAKE PEACE. By GEORGIANA M. CRAIK.

Peep at the Pixies (A), or LEGENDS OF THE WEST. By Mrs. BRAY.

Scenes and Stories of the Rhine. By M. BETHAM EDWARDS.

Seven Birthdays (The), or THE CHILDREN OF FORTUNE. By KATHLEEN KNOX.

Starlight Stories, TOLD TO BRIGHT EYES AND LISTENING EARS. By FANNY LABLACHE.

Stories of Edward, AND HIS LITTLE FRIENDS.

Tales of Magic and Meaning. Written and Illustrated by ALFRED CROWQUILL.

One Dollar Twenty-five Cents plain, cloth elegant, with Illustrations by eminent Artists, or with gilt edges, price One Dollar Fifty Cents.

Cast Adrift, the Story of a Waif. By Mrs. HERBERT MARTIN.

Castles and their Heroes. By BARBARA HUTTON.

Clement's Trial and Victory, or SOWING AND REAPING. By M. E. B. (Mrs. GELLIE). Third Thousand.

Faggots for the Fireside, or TALES OF FACT AND FANCY. By PETER PARLEY.

NEW AND POPULAR WORKS

One Dollar Twenty-five Cents each—continued.

Little May's Friends, or COUNTRY PETS AND PASTIMES. By ANNIE WHITTEM.

Louisa Broadhurst; or FIRST EXPERIENCES. By A. M.

My School Days in Paris. By MARGARET S. JEUNE.

Meadow Lea, or THE GIPSY CHILDREN.

Millicent and Her Cousins. By the Hon. AUGUSTA BETHELL.

New Girl (The), or THE RIVALS; a Tale of School Life. By M. E. B. (Mrs. GELLIE).

North Pole (The); AND HOW CHARLIE WILSON DISCOVERED IT. By the Author of "Realms of the Ice King," &c.

Our Old Uncle's Home; AND WHAT THE BOYS DID THERE. By Mother CAREY.

Queen Dora: THE LIFE AND LESSONS OF A LITTLE GIRL. By KATHLEEN KNOX.

Rosamond Fane, or THE PRISONERS OF ST. JAMES. By M. and C. LEE.

Talent in Tatters, or SOME VICISSITUDES IN THE LIFE OF AN ENGLISH BOY. By HOPE WRAYTHE.

The Triumphs of Steam, or STORIES FROM THE LIVES OF WATT ARKWRIGHT, AND STEPHENSON.

The Whispers of a Shell, or STORIES OF THE SEA. By FRANCES FREELING BRODERIP.

Wild Roses, or SIMPLE STORIES OF COUNTRY LIFE. By the same.

One Dollar each.

Great and Small; SCENES IN THE LIFE OF CHILDREN. Translated, with permission, from the French of Mdlle. Laroque, by Miss HARRIET POOLE. With 61 Illustrations by BERTALL.

Grey Towers; or AUNT HETTY'S WILL. By M. M. POLLARD.

Isabel's Difficulties, or LIGHT ON THE DAILY PATH. By M. R. CAREY.

Joachim's Spectacles: A LEGEND OF FLORENTHAL. By M. & C. LEE.

Kingston's (W.H.G.) Fred Markham in Russia, or, THE BOY TRAVELLERS IN THE LAND OF THE CZAR.

,, Manco the Peruvian Chief.

,, Mark Seaworth; a Tale of the Indian Ocean.

,, Peter the Whaler; HIS EARLY LIFE AND ADVENTURES IN THE ARCTIC REGIONS.

,, Salt Water, or NEIL D'ARCY'S SEA LIFE AND ADVENTURES.

One Dollar each—continued.

Lee (Mrs.) Anecdotes of the Habits and Instincts of Animals.
,, Anecdotes of the Habits and Instincts of Birds, Reptiles, and Fishes.
,, Adventures in Australia, or THE WANDERINGS OF CAPTAIN SPENCER IN THE BUSH AND THE WILDS.
,, The African Wanderers, or CARLOS AND ANTONIO.

One Dollar Twenty-five Cents each, cloth elegant, Illustrated.

Among the Zulus. By LIEUT-COL. DRAYSON. Cloth, gilt edges.
Attractive Picture Book (The). A New Gift Book from the Old Corner, containing numerous Illustrations by eminent Artists

> Bound in Elegant Paper Boards, Royal 4to, price $1·25. each plain; $2·00. coloured; $3·00. mounted on cloth and coloured.

Berries and Blossoms: a Verse Book for Young People. By T. WESTWOOD.
Bible Illustrations, or A DESCRIPTION OF MANNERS AND CUSTOMS PECULIAR TO THE EAST. By the Rev. B. H. DRAPER. Revised by Dr. KITTO.
British History Briefly Told (The), AND A DESCRIPTION OF THE ANCIENT CUSTOMS, SPORTS, AND PASTIMES OF THE ENGLISH.
Four Seasons (The); A Short Account of the Structure of Plants being Four Lectures written for the Working Men's Institute, Paris. With Illustrations. Imperial 16mo.
Family Bible Newly Opened (The); WITH UNCLE GOODWIN'S ACCOUNT OF IT. By JEFFREYS TAYLOR. Fcap. 8vo.
Glimpses of Nature, AND OBJECTS OF INTEREST DESCRIBED DURING A VISIT TO THE ISLE OF WIGHT. By Mrs. LOUDON. Forty-one Illustrations.
History of the Robins (The). By Mrs. TRIMMER. In Words of One Syllable. Edited by the Rev. CHARLES SWETE, M.A.
Historical Acting Charades, or AMUSEMENTS FOR WINTER EVENINGS. By the Author of "Cat and Dog," etc. Fcap. 8vo.
Infant Amusements, or HOW TO MAKE A NURSERY HAPPY. With Practical Hints on the Moral and Physical Training of Children. By W. H. G. KINGSTON.

18   NEW AND POPULAR WORKS

One Dollar Twenty-five Cents each—continued.

Man's Boot (The), AND OTHER STORIES IN WORDS OF ONE SYLLABLE. Illustrations by HARRISON WEIR. 4to., gilt edges.

The Mine, or SUBTERRANEAN WONDERS. An Account of the Operations of the Miner and the Products of his Labours.

Modern Sphinx (The). A Collection of ENIGMAS, CHARADES, REBUSES, DOUBLE AND TRIPLE ACROSTICS, ANAGRAMS, LOGOGRIPHS, METAGRAMS, VERBAL PUZZLES, CONUNDRUMS, etc. Fcap. 8vo.

Root and Flower. By JOHN PALMER.

Sunbeam: a Fairy Tale. By Mrs. PIETZKER.

Sylvia's New Home, a Story for the Young. By Mrs. J. F. B. FIRTH.

Taking Tales. Edited by W. H. G. KINGSTON. In Plain Language and Large Type. New Edition. Two vols.

May also be had in 4 vols, 50c. each; and 12 parts, 25c. and 20c. each.

One Dollar Twenty-five Cents plain; One Dollar Fifty Cents coloured.

Bear King (The): a Narrative confided to the Marines by JAMES GREENWOOD. With Illustrations by ERNEST GRISET. Small 4to.

Familiar Natural History. By Mrs. R. LEE. With 42 Illustrations by HARRISON WEIR.

* * * Also, in Two Vols., entitled "British Animals and Birds," "Foreign Animals and Birds." 75c. each, plain; $1·00. coloured.

Old Nurse's Book of Rhymes, Jingles, and Ditties. Illustrated by C. H. BENNETT. Ninety Engravings.

One Dollar, or gilt edges, One Dollar Twenty-five Cents.

Our Soldiers, or ANECDOTES OF THE CAMPAIGNS AND GALLANT DEEDS OF THE BRITISH ARMY DURING THE REIGN OF HER MAJESTY QUEEN VICTORIA. By W. H. G. KINGSTON. With Frontispiece. New and Revised Edition. Eighth Thousand.

Our Sailors, or ANECDOTES OF THE ENGAGEMENTS AND GALLANT DEEDS OF THE BRITISH NAVY. With Frontispiece. New and Revised Edition. Eighth Thousand.

Lucy's Campaign: a Story of Adventure. By M. and C. LEE. Gilt edges.

Fruits of Enterprise, EXHIBITED IN THE TRAVELS OF BELZONI IN EGYPT AND NUBIA. With Six Engravings by BIRKET FOSTER.

One Dollar each plain, Super Royal 16mo, cloth elegant, with Illustrations by Harrison Weir and others.

Adventures and Experiences of Biddy Dorking and of the Fat Frog. Edited by Mrs. S. C. HALL.

Alice and Beatrice. By GRANDMAMMA.

Amy's Wish, and What Came of It. By Mrs. TYLEE.

Animals and their Social Powers. By MARY TURNER-ANDREWES.

Cat and Dog, or MEMOIRS OF PUSS AND THE CAPTAIN.

Crib and Fly: a Tale of Two Terriers.

Discontented Children (The), AND HOW THEY WERE CURED. By M. and E. KIRBY.

Doll and Her Friends (The), or MEMOIRS OF THE LADY SERAPHINA. By the Author of "Cat and Dog."

Early Dawn (The), or STORIES TO THINK ABOUT.

Every Inch a King, or THE STORY OF REX AND HIS FRIENDS. By Mrs. J. WORTHINGTON BLISS.

Fairy Gifts, or A WALLET OF WONDERS. By KATHLEEN KNOX.

Funny Fables for Little Folks.

Fun and Earnest, or RHYMES WITH REASON. By D'ARCY W. THOMPSON. Illustrated by C. H. BENNETT. Imperial 16mo.

Gerty and May. Eighth Thousand.

By the same Author.

Granny's Story Box. New Edition. With 20 Engravings.

Children of the Parsonage.	**Sunny Days,** OR A MONTH AT
Our White Violet.	THE GREAT STOWE.

The New Baby.

Jack Frost and Betty Snow; with other Tales for Wintry Nights and Rainy Days.

Julia Maitland, or, PRIDE GOES BEFORE A FALL. BY M. & E. KIRBY.

Lost in the Jungle; A TALE OF THE INDIAN MUTINY. By AUGUSTA MARRYAT.

Madelon. By ESTHER CARR.

Neptune: or THE AUTOBIOGRAPHY OF A NEWFOUNDLAND DOG.

NEW AND POPULAR WORKS

One Dollar each—continued.

Norris (Emilia Marryat.) A Week by Themselves.
By the same Author.

Adrift on the Sea.	Seaside Home.
Children's Pic-Nic (The).	Snowed Up.
Geoffry's Great Fault.	Stolen Cherries.
Harry at School.	What became of Tommy.
Paul Howard's Captivity.	

Odd Stories about Animals: told in Short and Easy Words.

Our Home in the Marsh Land, or DAYS OF AULD LANG SYNE. By E. L. F.

Scripture Histories for Little Children. With Sixteen Illustrations by JOHN GILBERT.
> CONTENTS:—The History of Joseph—History of Moses—History of our Saviour—The Miracles of Christ.
> *Sold separately 25c. each, plain; 50c. coloured.*

Secret of Wrexford (The), or STELLA DESMOND'S SECRET. By ESTHER CARR.

Stories of Julian and His Playfellows. Written by his MAMMA.

Tales from Catland. Dedicated to the Young Kittens of England. By an OLD TABBY. Seventh Thousand.

Talking Bird (The), or THE LITTLE GIRL WHO KNEW WHAT WAS GOING TO HAPPEN. By M. and E. KIRBY.

Ten of Them, or THE CHILDREN OF DANEHURST. By Mrs. R. M. BRAY.

"Those Unlucky Twins!" By A. LYSTER.

Tiny Stories for Tiny Readers in Tiny Words.

Tittle Tattle; and other Stories for Children. By the Author of "Little Tales for Tiny Tots," etc.

Trottie's Story Book: True Tales in Short Words and Large Type.

Tuppy, or THE AUTOBIOGRAPHY OF A DONKEY.

Wandering Blindfold, or A BOY'S TROUBLES. By MARY ALBERT.

One Dollar Twenty-five Cents with Illustrations, cloth elegant, or with gilt edges, One Dollar Fifty Cents.

A Child's Influence, or KATHLEEN AND HER GREAT UNCLE. By LISA LOCKYER.

Adventures of Kwei, the Chinese Girl. By M.E.B. (Mrs. GELLIE).

One Dollar each—continued.

Bertrand Du Guesclin, the Hero of Brittany. By EMILE DE BONNECHOSE. Translated by MARGARET S. JEUNE.
Corner Cottage, and Its Inmates, or TRUST IN GOD. By FRANCES OSBORNE.
Davenport's (Mrs.) Constance and Nellie, or THE LOST WILL.
,,   Our Birthdays, AND HOW TO IMPROVE THEM.
,,   The Holidays Abroad, or RIGHT AT LAST.
Father Time's Story Book for the Little Ones. By KATHLEEN KNOX.
From Peasant to Prince, or THE LIFE OF ALEXANDER PRINCE MENSCHIKOFF. From the Russian by Madame PIETZKER.
William Allair, or RUNNING AWAY TO SEA. By Mrs. H. WOOD.

One Dollar each, Illustrated.

Among the Zulus: the Adventures of Hans Sterk, South African Hunter and Pioneer. By LIEUT.-COLONEL A. W. DRAYSON, R.A.
Boy's Own Toy Maker (The): a Practical Illustrated Guide to the useful employment of Leisure Hours. By E. LANDELLS. 200 Illustrations.
Girl's Own Toy Maker (The), AND BOOK OF RECREATION. By E. and A. LANDELLS. With 200 Illustrations.
Little Child's Fable Book. Arranged Progressively in One, Two and Three Syllables. 16 Page Illus. ($1.50 *coloured, gilt edges.*)
Little Pilgrim (The). Revised and Illustrated by HELEN PETRIE.
Model Yachts, and Model Yacht Sailing: HOW TO BUILD, RIG, AND SAIL A SELF-ACTING MODEL YACHT. By JAS. E. WALTON, V.M.Y.C. Fcap. 4to., with 58 Woodcuts.
Silly Peter: A QUEER STORY OF A DAFT BOY, A PRINCE, AND A MILLER'S DAUGHTER. By W. NORRIS.
Spring Time; or, Words in Season. A Book for Girls. By SIDNEY COX. Third Edition.

A NEW UNIFORM SERIES OF ONE-DOLLAR BOOKS.
Cloth elegant, fully Illustrated.

African Pets: or, CHATS ABOUT OUR ANIMAL FRIENDS IN NATAL, WITH A SKETCH OF KAFFIR LIFE. By F. CLINTON PARRY.
Bunchy: or, THE CHILDREN OF SCARSBROOK FARM. By Miss E. C. PHILLIPS, Author of "The Orphans," &c.
Ways and Tricks of Animals, WITH STORIES ABOUT AUNT MARY'S PETS. By MARY HOOPER.
Kitty and Bo: or, THE STORY OF A VERY LITTLE GIRL AND BOY. By A. T. With Frontispiece.
On the Leads: or, WHAT THE PLANETS SAW. By Mrs. A. A. STRANGE BUTSON.

COMICAL PICTURE BOOKS.

One Dollar each, Coloured Plates, fancy boards.

English Struwwelpeter (The): or PRETTY STORIES AND FUNNY PICTURES FOR LITTLE CHILDREN. After the celebrated German Work, Dr. HEINRICH HOFFMANN, Twenty-sixth Edition. Twenty-four pages of Illustrations (or mounted on linen, $1·50).

Funny Picture Book (The); or, 25 FUNNY LITTLE LESSONS. A free translation from the German of "DER KLEINE, A.B.C. SCHÜTZ."

Loves of Tom Tucker and Little Bo-Peep. Written and Illustrated by THOMAS HOOD.

Spectropia, or SURPRISING SPECTRAL ILLUSIONS, showing Ghosts everywhere, and of any Colour. By J. H. BROWN.

Upside Down: a Series of Amusing Pictures from Sketches by the late W. MCCONNELL, with Verses by THOMAS HOOD.

Seventy-five Cents cloth elegant, with Illustrations, or with coloured plates, gilt edges, One Dollar.

Fanny and Her Mamma, or EASY LESSONS FOR CHILDREN.

Good in Everything, or THE EARLY HISTORY OF GILBERT HARLAND. By Mrs. BARWELL.

Infantine Knowledge: a Spelling and Reading Book on a Popular Plan.

Little Lessons for Little Learners, in Words of One Syllable. By Mrs. BARWELL.

Mamma's Bible Stories, FOR HER LITTLE BOYS AND GIRLS.

Mamma's Bible Stories (A Sequel to).

Mamma's Lessons, FOR HER LITTLE BOYS AND GIRLS.

Silver Swan (The): a Fairy Tale. By MADAME DE CHATELAIN.

Tales of School Life. By AGNES LOUDON.

Wonders of Home, in Eleven Stories (The). By GRANDFATHER GREY.

Seventy-five Cents each.

Confessions of a Lost Dog (The). Reported by her Mistress, FRANCES POWER COBBE. With a Photograph of the Dog from Life, by FRANK HAES.

Home Amusements: a Choice Collection of Riddles, Charades, Conundrums, Parlour Games, and Forfeits.

How to Make Dolls' Furniture AND TO FURNISH A DOLL'S HOUSE. With 70 Illustrations. Small 4to.

PUBLISHED BY E. P. DUTTON AND CO.   23

Seventy-five Cents each—continued.

Illustrated Paper Model Maker. By E. LANDELLS.

Rhymes and Pictures ABOUT BREAD, TEA, SUGAR, COTTON, COALS, AND GOLD. By WILLIAM NEWMAN. Seventy-two Illustrations. Price 75c. *plain;* $1.25 *coloured.*

⁂ Each Subject may be had separately. 20c. *plain;* 40c. *coloured.*

Scenes of Animal Life and Character, FROM NATURE AND RECOLLECTION. In Twenty Plates. By J. B. 4to, fancy boards.

Surprising Adventures of the Clumsy Boy Crusoe (The). By CHARLES H. ROSS. With Twenty-three Coloured Illustrations.

A NEW UNIFORM SERIES.

Price Fifty Cents each, cloth elegant, fully Illustrated.

Angelo; or, THE PINE FOREST IN THE ALPS. By GERALDINE E. JEWSBURY. 5th Thousand.

Aunt Annette's Stories to Ada. By ANNETTE A. SALAMAN.

Brave Nelly; or, WEAK HANDS AND A WILLING HEART. By M.E.B (Mrs. GELLIE). Fifth Thousand.

Featherland; or, HOW THE BIRDS LIVED AT GREENLAWN. By G. M. FENN. 4th Thousand.

Humble Life: a Tale of HUMBLE HOMES. By the Author of "Gerty and May," &c.

Kingston's (W. H. G.) Child of the Wreck: or, THE LOSS OF THE ROYAL GEORGE.

Lee's (Mrs. R.) Playing at Settlers; or, THE FAGGOT HOUSE.

———— Twelve Stories of the Sayings and Doings of Animals.

Little Lisette, THE ORPHAN OF ALSACE. By M.E.B. (Mrs. GELLIE).

Live Toys; OR, ANECDOTES OF OUR FOUR-LEGGED AND OTHER PETS. By EMMA DAVENPORT.

Long Evenings; or, STORIES FOR MY LITTLE FRIENDS. By EMILIA MARRYATT.

Three Wishes (The). By M.E.B. (Mrs. GELLIE).

Price Fifty Cents each, cloth elegant, Illustrated.

Always Happy, or, ANECDOTES OF FELIX AND HIS SISTER SERENA. By a Mother. Twentieth Thousand.

Every-Day Things, or USEFUL KNOWLEDGE RESPECTING THE PRINCIPAL ANIMAL, VEGETABLE, AND MINERAL SUBSTANCES IN COMMON USE.

Grandmamma's Relics, AND HER STORIES ABOUT THEM. By E. E. BOWEN.

Happy Holidays: or, BROTHERS AND SISTERS AT HOME. By EMMA DAVENPORT. New and cheaper Edition.

Holiday Tales. By FLORENCE WILFORD. Author of "Nigel Bartram's Ideal," etc.

Kingston (W. H. G.) The Heroic Wife; or, THE ADVENTURES OF A FAMILY ON THE BANKS OF THE AMAZON.

Little Roebuck (The), from the German. Illustrated by LOSSON. Fancy boards (75c. *coloured*).

Taking Tales. Edited by W. H. G. KINGSTON. In Plain Language and Large Type. Four vols.

May also be had in Two vols., $1·25 each; and in 12 parts, paper covers, price 20c. each; or cloth limp, 25c. each.

Trimmer's (Mrs.) New Testament Lessons. With 40 Engravings.

A NEW UNIFORM SERIES OF FORTY-CENT VOLUMES.

Cloth elegant, Illustrated.

Among the Brigands, and other Tales of Adventure. New and cheaper Edition. Fourth Thousand.

Christian Elliott: or, MRS. DANVER'S PRIZE. By L. N. COMYN. New and cheaper Edition. Fourth Thousand.

Wrecked, Not Lost; or THE PILOT AND HIS COMPANION. By the Hon. Mrs. DUNDAS. New and cheaper Edition. Fifth Thousand.

THE FAVOURITE LIBRARY.

New Editions of the Volumes in this Series are being issued, and other Volumes by Popular Authors will be added.

Cloth elegant, with coloured frontispiece and title-page, Forty Cents each.

1. The Eskdale Herd Boy. By LADY STODDART.
2. Mrs. Leicester's School. By CHARLES and MARY LAMB.
3. The History of The Robins. By MRS. TRIMMER.
4. Memoir of Bob, The Spotted Terrier.
5. Keeper's Travels in Search of His Master.
6. The Scottish Orphans. By LADY STODDART.
7. Never Wrong; or, the Young Disputant; & It was only in Fun.
8. The Life and Perambulations of a Mouse.
9. The Son of a Genius. By MRS. HOFLAND.
10. The Daughter of a Genius. By MRS. HOFLAND.
11. Ellen, the Teacher. By MRS. HOFLAND.
12. Theodore; or, The Crusaders. By MRS. HOFLAND.
13. Right and Wrong. By the Author of "ALWAYS HAPPY."
14. Harry's Holiday. By JEFFERYS TAYLOR.
15. Short Poems and Hymns for Children.

Price Fifty Cents each, in various styles of binding.

The Picturesque Primer.
Fragments of Knowledge for Little Folk.
Easy Reading for Little Readers.
The Nursery Companion.

These Four Volumes contain about 450 pictures. Each one being complete in itself, and bound in an attractive paper cover (also with coloured Illustrations, 50c.)

The Four Volumes bound together form the "Favourite Picture Book," bound in cloth, price $2·00, or coloured Illustrations, gilt edges, $4·00.

Australian Babes in the Wood (The): a True Story told in Rhyme for the Young. Price 40c. boards, 50c. cloth, gilt edges.

Cowslip (The). Fully Illustrated cloth, 40c. *plain;* 50c. *coloured.*

Daisy (The). Fully Illustrated cloth, 40c *plain;* 50c. *coloured.*

Dame Partlett's Farm. AN ACCOUNT OF THE RICHES SHE OBTAINED BY INDUSTRY, &c. Coloured Illustrations, sewed.

Female Christian Names, AND THEIR TEACHINGS. A Gift Book for Girls. By MARY E. BROMFIELD. Cloth, gilt edges.

Fifty Cents each—continued.

Golden Words for Children, FROM THE BOOK OF LIFE. In English, French, and German. A set of Illuminated Cards in Packet. Or bound in cloth interleaved, price $1·00 gilt edges.

Goody Two Shoes: or THE HISTORY OF LITTLE MARGERY MEANWELL IN RHYME. Fully Illustrated, cloth.

Hand Shadows, to be thrown upon the Wall. Novel and amusing figures formed by the hand. By HENRY BURSILL. New and cheaper Edition. Twelfth. Thousand. Two Series in one. (Or coloured Illustrations, 75c.)

Headlong Career (The) and Woeful Ending of Precocious Piggy. By THOMAS HOOD. Illustrated by his Son. Printed in colours. Fancy wrapper, 4to. (Or mounted on cloth, untearable, 75c.)

Johnny Miller; OR TRUTH AND PERSEVERANCE. By FELIX WEISS.

Nine Lives of a Cat (The): a Tale of Wonder. Written and Illustrated by C. H. BENNETT. 24 Coloured Engravings, sewed.

Peter Piper. PRACTICAL PRINCIPLES OF PLAIN AND PERFECT PRONUNCIATION. Coloured Illustrations, sewed.

Plaiting Pictures. A NOVEL PASTIME BY WHICH CHILDREN CAN CONSTRUCT AND RECONSTRUCT PICTURES FOR THEMSELVES. Four Series in Fancy Coloured Wrappers. Oblong 4to.
First Series.—Juvenile Party—Zoological Gardens—The Gleaner.
Second Series.—Birds' Pic-nic—Cats' Concert—Three Bears.
Third Series.—Blind Man's Buff—Children in the Wood—Snow Man.
Fourth Series.—Grandfather's Birthday—Gymnasium—Playroom.

Primrose Pilgrimage (The): a Woodland Story. By M. BETHAM EDWARDS. Illustrated by MACQUOID. Sewed.

Short and Simple Prayers, with Hymns for the Use of Children. By the Author of "Mamma's Bible Stories." Sixteenth Thousand. Cloth.

Whittington and his Cat. Coloured Illustrations, sewed.

Young Vocalist (The). A Collection of Twelve Songs, each with an Accompaniment for the Pianoforte. By Mrs. MOUNSEY BARTHOLOMEW. New and Cheaper Edition. (Or bound in cloth, price 75c.)

DURABLE NURSERY BOOKS.

Mounted on cloth with coloured plates, Fifty Cents each.

1. COCK ROBIN.
2. COURTSHIP OF JENNY WREN.
3. DAME TROT AND HER CAT.
4. HOUSE THAT JACK BUILT
5. PUSS IN BOOTS.

Price 30c. each, elegantly bound in Paper Boards.

THE TINY NATURAL HISTORY SERIES.

ALL THE VOLUMES ARE PROFUSELY ILLUSTRATED BY THE BEST ARTISTS.

Little Nellie's Bird Cage. By Mrs. R. LEE. Author of "The African Wanderers," &c.

The Tiny Menagerie. By Mrs. R. LEE. Author of "The African Wanderers," &c.

The Dog Postman. By the Author of "Odd Stories."

The Mischievous Monkey. By the Author of "Odd Stories."

Lily's Letters from the Farm. By MARY HOOPER. Author of "Ways and Tricks of Animals."

Our Dog Prin. By MARY HOOPER. Author of "Ways and Tricks of Animals."

Little Neddie's Menagerie. By Mrs. R. LEE. Author of "The African Wanderers," &c.

Frolicsome Frisk and his Friends. By the Author of "Trottie's Story Book."

Wise Birds and Clever Dogs. By the Author of "Tuppy," "Tiny Stories," &c.

Artful Pussy. By the Author of "Odd Stories," &c.

The Pet Pony. By the Author of "Trottie's Story Book."

Bow Wow Bobby. By the Author of "Tuppy," "Odd Stories," &c.

In 12 Parts, cloth limp, fancy binding, with Chromo on side. Price Twenty-five Cents.

TAKING TALES.

Edited by W. H. G. KINGSTON. Fully illustrated.

N.B.—Each Tale is Illustrated and complete in itself.

1. The Miller of Hillbrook: A RURAL TALE.
2. Tom Trueman, A SAILOR IN A MERCHANTMAN.
3. Michael Hale and his Family in Canada.
4. John Armstrong, THE SOLDIER.
5. Joseph Rudge, THE AUSTRALIAN SHEPHERD.
6. Life Underground; OR DICK, THE COLLIERY BOY.
7. Life on the Coast; OR THE LITTLE FISHER GIRL.
8. Adventures of Two Orphans in London.
9. Early Days on Board a Man-of-War.
10. Walter, the Foundling: A TALE OF OLDEN TIMES.
11. The Tenants of Sunnyside Farm.
12. Holmwood; OR, THE NEW ZEALAND SETTLER.

N.B.—May also be had in 4 vols. 50c. each, and 2 vols. $1.25. each.

Price Twenty-five Cents each, Plain ; Fifty Cents coloured.

ILLUSTRATED BY HARRISON WEIR AND JOHN GILBERT.

1. British Animals. 1st Series.
2. British Animals. 2nd Series.
3. British Birds.
4. Foreign Animals. 1st Series.
5. Foreign Animals. 2nd Series.
6. Foreign Birds.
7. The Farm and its Scenes.
8. The diverting history of John Gilpin.
9. The Peacock at home, and Butterfly's Ball.
10. History of Joseph.
11. History of Moses.
12. Life of our Saviour.
13. Miracles of Christ.

His name was Hero. Price 50c. sewed.

By the Same Author.

How I became a Governess. 3rd Edit. 75c. cloth ; $1·00 gilt edges.
My Pretty Puss. With Frontispiece. Price 25c.
The Grateful Sparrow : a True Story. Fifth Edition. Price 25c.
The Adventures of a Butterfly Price 40c.

The Hare that Found his Way Home. Price 25c.

WORKS FOR DISTRIBUTION.

A Woman's Secret ; or, How to Make Home Happy. Thirty-third Thousand. 18mo, price 25c.

By the same Author, uniform in size and price.

Woman's Work ; or, How she can Help the Sick. 19th Thousand.

A Chapter of Accidents ; or, The Mother's Assistant in Cases of Burns, Scalds, Cuts, &c. Ninth Thousand.

Pay to-day, Trust to-morrow ; illustrating the Evils of the Tally System. Seventh Thousand.

Nursery Work ; or, Hannah Baker's First Place. Fifth Thousand.

The Cook and the Doctor ; or, Cheap Recipes and Useful Remedies. Selected from the three first books.

Home Difficulties. A Few Words on the Servant Question.

Family Prayers for Cottage Homes.

Educational Works.

HISTORY.

Britannia : a Collection of the Principal Passages in Latin Authors that refer to this Island, with Vocabulary and Notes. By T. S. Cayzer. Illustrated with a Map and 29 Woodcuts. Crown 8vo. Price $1·25.

True Stories from Ancient History, chronologically arranged from the Creation of the World to the Death of Charlemagne. 12mo. $1·50.

HISTORY—*continued*.

Mrs. Trimmer's Concise History of England, revised and brought down to the present Time. By Mrs. MILNER. With Portraits of the Sovereigns. $1·50.

Rhymes of Royalty: the History of England in Verse, from the Norman Conquest to the reign of VICTORIA; with a summary of the leading events in each reign. Fcap. 8vo. 75c.

GEOGRAPHY.

Glimpses of the Globe. A First Geographical Reader for Children. By J. R. BLAKISTON, Author of "The Teacher," &c., 40c.

Pictorial Geography, for the Instruction of Young Children. Price 50c.; mounted on rollers, $1·25.

Gaultier's Familiar Geography. With a concise Treatise on the Artificial Sphere, and two coloured Maps, illustrative of the principal Geographical Terms. 16mo. $1·00.

Butler's Outline Maps, and Key, or GEOGRAPHICAL AND BIOGRAPHICAL EXERCISES; with a Set of Coloured Outline Maps, designed for the use of Young Persons. By the late WILLIAM BUTLER. Enlarged by the Author's Son, J. O. BUTLER. Thirty-sixth Edition. Revised, $1·50.

GRAMMAR, &c.

A Compendious Grammar, AND PHILOLOGICAL HAND-BOOK OF THE ENGLISH LANGUAGE, for the use of Schools and Candidates for the Army and Civil Service Examinations. By J. G. COLQUHOUN, Esq., Barrister-at-Law. Fcap. 8vo. Cloth, $1·00.

Darnell, G. Grammar made Intelligible to Children. Being a Series of short and simple Rules, with ample Explanations of Every Difficulty, and copious Exercises for Parsing; in Language adapted to the comprehension of very Young Students. New and Revised Edition. Cloth, 50c.

Darnell, G. Introduction to English Grammar. Price 15c. Being the first 32 pages of "Grammar made Intelligible."

Darnell, T. Parsing Simplified: an Introduction and Companion to all Grammars; consisting of Short and Easy Rules, with Parsing Lessons to each. Price 50c.

Lovechilds, Mrs. The Child's Grammar. 50th Edition. 40c. cloth.

A Word to the Wise, or HINTS ON THE CURRENT IMPROPRIETIES OF EXPRESSION IN WRITING AND SPEAKING. By PARRY GWYNNE. Sixteenth Thousand. 18mo, price 25c. sewed; or 50c. cloth, gilt edges.

Harry Hawkins's H-Book; showing how he learned to aspirate his H's. Eighth Thousand. Sewed, price 25c.

Prince of Wales's Primer (The). With 340 Illustrations by J. GILBERT. Price 25c.

GRAMMAR—continued.

Darnell, G. Short and Certain Road to Reading. Being a Series EASY LESSONS in which the Alphabet is so divided as to enable the Child to read many pages of Familiar Phrases before he has learned half the letters. Cloth, 25c.; or in Four parts, paper covers, 5c. each.

Sheet Lessons. Being Extracts from the above, printed in very large, bold type. Price, for the Set of Six Sheets, 25c.; or, neatly mounted on boards, $1·00.

ARITHMETIC AND ALGEBRA.

Darnell, G. Arithmetic made Intelligible to Children. Being a Series of GRADUALLY ADVANCING EXERCISES, intended to employ the Reason rather than the Memory of the Pupil; with ample Explanations of Every Difficulty, in Language adapted to the comprehension of very young Students. Cloth, 50c.

⁎ This work may be had in Three parts—Part I., price 25c. Part II., price 30c. Part III., price 25c. A KEY to Parts II and III., price 50c. (Part I. does not require a Key.)

Cayzer, T. S. One Thousand Arithmetical Tests, or THE EXAMINER'S ASSISTANT. Specially adapted, by a novel arrangement of the subject, for Examination Purposes, but also suited for general use in Schools. With a complete set of Examples and Models of Work. Price 75c.

Key with Solutions of all the Examples in the One Thousand Arithmetical Tests. Price $1·50. cloth. The Answers only, price 75c. cloth.

One Thousand Algebraical Tests; on the same plan. 8vo, price $1·00. cloth.

ANSWERS to the Algebraical Tests, price $1·00

Theory and Practice of the Metric System of Weights and Measures. By Prof. LEONE LEVI, F.S.A., F.S.S. Sewed 50c.

Essentials of Geometry, Plane and Solid (The), as taught in Germany and France. By J. R. MORELL. Numerous Diagrams. 75c. cloth.

Artizan Cookery and How to Teach it. By a Pupil of the National Training School for Cookery, South Kensington. Sewed, price 25c.

ELEMENTARY FRENCH AND GERMAN WORKS.

L'Abécédaire of French Pronunciation: A Manual for Teachers and Students. By G. LEPRÉVOST, of Paris, Professor of Languages. Crown 8vo., cloth, 75c.

Le Babillard: an Amusing Introduction to the French Language. By a FRENCH LADY Ninth Edition. 16 Plates. 75c. cloth.

Les Jeunes Narrateurs, ou PETITS CONTES MORAUX. With a Key to the difficult Words and Phrases. 3rd Edition. 75c. cloth.

ELEMENTARY WORKS, &c.—*continued*

Pictorial French Grammar (The). For the use of Children. By MARIN DE LA VOYE. With 80 Illus. Royal 16mo, 50c. cloth.

Rowbotham's New and Easy Method of Learning the French Genders. New Edition. 25c.

Bellenger's French Word and Phrase Book; containing a select Vocabulary and Dialogues. New Edition. Price 50c.

Der Schwätzer, or THE PRATTLER. An Amusing Introduction to the German Language. Sixteen Illustrations. Price 75c. cloth.

NEEDLEWORK.

By the Examiner of Needlework to the School Board for London.

Plain Hints for those who have to Examine Needlework, whether for Government Grants, Prize Associations, or Local Managers, to which is added Skeleton Demonstration Lessons to be used with the Demonstration Frames, and a glossary of terms used in the Needlework required from the scholars in public elementary schools. Price 75c.

NEEDLEWORK DEMONSTRATION SHEETS

Exhibit, by Diagrams and Descriptions, the formation of Stitches in Elementary Needlework. The size of the Sheets is 30 × 22 inches. Price, 50c. each; or, mounted on rollers and varnished, $1·00.

Whip Stitch for Frills, and Fern or Coral Stitch ... 1 Sheet	Grafting Stocking Material... 1 Sheet
Hemming, Seaming, and Stitching ... ... 1 ,,	Stocking Web Stitch... ... 1 ,,
Button Hole ... ... 1 ,,	True Marking Stitch... ... 1 ,,
Fisherman's Stitch for Braiding Nets ... ... 1 ,,	Alphabets for Marking ... 6 ,,
Herring Bone ... ... 1 ,,	Setting in Gathers or "Stocking" Knotting or Seeding (English Method) ... ... 1 ,,

The Demonstration Frame for Class Teaching, with Special Needle and Cord. Price complete, $2·00.

Plain Needlework arranged in Six Standards, with Hints for the Management of Classes, and Appendix on Simultaneous Teaching. Nineteenth Thousand. Price 25c.

Plain Knitting and Mending arranged in Six Standards, with 20 Diagrams. Twelfth Thousand. Price 25c.

Plain Cutting Out for Standards IV., V., and VI., as now required by the Government Educational Department. Adapted to the principles of Elementary Geometry. Sixth Thousand. Price 50c.

A set of the **Diagrams** referred to in the book may be had separately, printed on stout paper and enclosed in an envelope. Price 50c.

⁎ *These works are recommended in the published Code of the Educational Department.*

Needlework, Schedule III. Exemplified and Illustrated. Intended for the use of Young Teachers and of the Upper Standards in Elementary Schools. By Mrs. E. A. CURTIS. Cloth limp, with 30 Illustrations, 5th Thousand, price 50c.

PUBLICATIONS BY E. P. DUTTON AND CO.

DARNELL'S COPY-BOOKS

FOR BOARD, PRIVATE, & PUBLIC SCHOOLS.

Adapted to the Grades of the New Educational Code.

DARNELL'S LARGE POST COPY-BOOKS,
16 Nos., 25c. each.

The first ten of which have, on every alternate line, appropriate and carefully-written copies in Pencil-coloured Ink, to be first written over and then imitated, the remaining numbers having Black Head-lines for imitation only, THE WHOLE GRADUALLY ADVANCING FROM A SIMPLE STROKE TO A SUPERIOR SMALL HAND.

DARNELL'S FOOLSCAP COPY-BOOKS,
24 Nos., oblong, on the same plan; or, Superior Paper, Marble Covers.

DARNELL'S UNIVERSAL COPY-BOOKS,
16 Nos., on the same plan.

DARNELL'S COPY-BOOKS are the oldest and best.

DARNELL'S COPY-BOOKS are a sure guide to a good handwriting.

DARNELL'S COPY-BOOKS have enjoyed over a quarter of a century of public favour.

DARNELL'S COPY-BOOKS are used in nearly all the best Schools in Great Britain and the Colonies.

DARNELL'S COPY-BOOKS are the production of an experienced schoolmaster.

DARNELL'S COPY-BOOKS gradually advance from the simple stroke to a superior small hand.

DARNELL'S COPY-BOOKS.—The assistance given in the primal lessons is reduced as the learner progresses, until all guidance is safely withdrawn.

DARNELL'S COPY-BOOKS.—The number and variety of the copies secure attention, and prevent the pupils copying their own writing, as in books with single head-lines.

DARNELL'S COPY-BOOKS ensure the progress of the learner, and greatly lighten the labours of the teacher.

DARNELL'S COPY-BOOKS.—Important Testimony:—"For teaching writing, I would recommend the use of Darnell's Copy-Books. I have noticed a marked improvement wherever they have been used."—Report of Mr. MAYE (National Society's Organiser of Schools) to the Worcester Diocesan Board of Education.

SPECIMEN COPIES of any of the above will be sent post free on receipt of stamps or Post-office order.

EDUCATIONAL AND OTHER CATALOGUES sent post free on application.

E. P. DUTTON & Co., NEW YORK.

www.ingramcontent.com/pod-product-compliance
Lightning Source LLC
Chambersburg PA
CBHW020243170426
43202CB00008B/202